JESUS AND HIS PARABLES

Behold, a virgin shall be with child, and shall bring forth a son, and they shall call his name Emmanuel, which being interpreted is, God with us.

JESUS AND HIS PARABLES

BY

J. ALEXANDER FINDLAY
M.A., D.D.

LONDON: THE EPWORTH PRESS

PUBLISHED BY
THE EPWORTH PRESS
(FRANK H. CUMBERS)
25–35 CITY ROAD, LONDON, E.C.1

*

New York . Toronto
Melbourne . Cape Town

*

Made in Great Britain
First published in 1950
Reprinted 1951
Reprinted 1957

Published for the
Fernley-Hartley Trust

Reproduced by photo-lithography and made at the Pitman Press, Bath

PREFACE

THIS STUDY in the Parables of our Lord has been inspired by its author's growing feeling that the best modern evangelical theology is in real danger of creating a new kind of Pharisaism, interested in Christian ideas, such as the doctrine of the Church or the 'theology of crisis', rather than in common earthly men and women. The denunciation of 'humanism' has perhaps gone on long enough; by this time it is surely common ground among thoughtful men that human nature cannot help itself, that necessary evolutionary progress is a delusion, and that it is one of the Christian preacher's tasks to shatter the last remains of *laisser-faire* in religion as it has been shattered in political and economic thought. But the question still meets us, as we turn back from the Epistle to the Romans to the parables of Jesus: why is there little or nothing of all this in them? Why are they so completely different as they show themselves to be when we look at them with eyes clear of traditional morals imposed upon them, from all other stories told for edification by pious people? There must be a reason, and we *must* find what it is, for 'Make yourselves friends of the mammon of unrighteousness' is as much part of the Word of God as 'Except you repent, you shall all likewise perish'. Why are the parables of Jesus so little like our sermons or devotional manuals, with an obvious evangelical application and intent? The question clamours to be answered. Is it perhaps that Jesus wishes to make us first observers of what God is doing, and only then moralists pointing out what should be done? My very numerous quotations from the Gospels are taken direct from the original, and I am responsible for the faults of the rendering offered. My debts to others are too many and far-reaching to be written down in a sentence; no one who knows anything about me will fail to know how great they are, and to whom they are chiefly due.

J. ALEXANDER FINDLAY

CONTENTS

CHAPTER ONE

WHAT CONSTITUTES A PARABLE?

One's natural inclination on being asked this question is to turn to the Old Testament, for Old and New Testaments are two volumes of the same Book, nor can anything in one be completely understood without the other. But it must be confessed that in this instance the Old Testament use of the word or words translated 'parable' or 'proverb' in our versions is not so illuminating as usual. The Hebrew word '*mashal*' has many meanings, and is translated in our versions by words so different in sense as 'parable' and 'proverb' (as for instance in 'Balaam took up his parable' (Numbers 23[7]) and the title of the Book of Proverbs). This ambiguity is reflected in the New Testament, where the Greek words '*parabolē*' and '*paroimia*' (proverb) are both used, the former in the Synoptics, the latter in the Fourth Gospel (John 10[6], 16[25, 29]).

Old Testament passages such as Numbers 23[7], Job 27[1] and 29[1] suggest that the phrase 'take up one's parable' is used to denote impassioned poetic speech like the 'hwyl' once so often heard at preaching-meetings in Wales. Balaam under prophetic inspiration soared into poetry rising to a dithyrambic rhythm both of intonation and form. As Moffatt shows in his translation of the New Testament, Jesus in speech and Paul in writing both manifest this tendency; good examples of which may be found in the Sermon on the Mount or in Romans 8, 1 Corinthians 13 and 15. 'Parable' here cannot be merely synonymous with 'prophecy', for 'prophecy' might apply to Balaam, but scarcely to Job. One example in Ezekiel (17[2ff.]) reminds us more closely of the parables of Jesus. Another (24[3ff.]) is what we should call an acted parable. Of such there are perhaps no examples in the Synoptic Gospels, though Mark 11[12ff.] (the so-called 'cursing of the fig-tree') has sometimes—mistakenly, I think—been interpreted in this way. An indubitable example of this method of teaching appears, however, in the newly discovered 'Egerton' papyrus Gospel-fragment (dated by the experts before A.D. 150), C. H. Dodd's reconstruction of which may be translated: 'Jesus stood on the bank of the Jordan river and, stretching out His right hand, filled it with water and broadcast it on the shore; then He made the earth wet with the water He had shaken over it, and it was absorbed in the soil as He stood there, and brought forth fruit.' This looks very much like an illustration by means of an acted parable of the question which appears in the first three lines of the fragment: 'When a farmer hides a little seed in a secret place, and it is not clear how the seed is dispersed, how does it come to possess its weight exceeding that of the seed from which it comes immeasurably?' In a certain sense, moreover (and this is, of course, true especially of the Fourth Gospel), many miracles of Jesus may rightly be described as acted parables, and it is clear that parables and miracles ought to be studied together far more closely than has generally been customary. The meaning 'proverb' occurs in Luke 4^{23} ('Doubtless ye will say unto me this parable, Physician, heal thyself') and in 2 Peter 2^{22}; these examples corresponding exactly to 1 Samuel 10^{12} ('Is Saul also among the prophets?') and 24^{13}. (See also Ezekiel $12^{22f.}$, $18^{2f.}$.) Closely connected with this usage is the appearance of the word 'parable' as a synonym for 'byword' in Deuteronomy 28^{37}, 1 Kings 9^{7}, 2 Chronicles 7^{20}, Psalm 69^{11}, and Ezekiel 14^{8}—there seems to be no exact parallel to this usage in the New Testament. The meaning 'dirge' and 'taunting-song' found in Micah 2^{4} and Habakkuk 2^{6} (translated here 'parable') and in Isaiah 14^{4} ('parable') should be mentioned—Jeremiah 24^{9} suggesting that this meaning was derived from that of 'byword'. In Habakkuk 2^{6}, where 'parable' and 'taunting proverb' come together, our official translators show that they thought *mashal* ('parable') and *chidah* ('taunting proverb') synonymous.

It was remarked above that the Fourth evangelist uses the Greek word '*paroimia*', which means '*obiter dictum*', a proverbial saying which has become, as we say, 'a household word' in contexts in which the Synoptic Gospels would lead us to expect '*parabolē*', e.g. John 10^{6}, $16^{25, 29}$. The Revisers of 1881 have misled us here, for they allowed 'parable' to appear in 10^{6}, and 'proverbs' in the other two places.

It will clear the way for our discussion of the meaning of the word 'parable' in the Synoptic Gospels if we deal with the Johannine use of '*paroimia*' at once. As we have seen, our versions take it as, to all intents and purposes, a synonym for '*parabolē*', and indeed some of the Old Testament passages cited above seem to bear this out. But such a cursory treatment of this subject does not do justice to the fact, which is surely not without significance, that the Synoptics invariably choose one word and the Fourth evangelist the other. What, then, is a 'proverb' as distinct from a 'parable'? Generally rather a saying than a narrative—a word spoken, as the Greek word '*paroimia*' suggests, by the wayside. The meaning 'dark saying', given to it by so many commentators on the Fourth Gospel, is found nowhere else in Greek literature —perhaps the fact that they have had to invent a new meaning for '*paroimia*' is merely due to its confusion with '*parabolē*', which appears to have the meaning of 'dark saying' in such passages as Matthew 13^{35} (quoted from Psalm 78^{2}) and perhaps in Mark 4^{11}. But household words like those found in the Book of Proverbs cannot be called dark sayings—their chief characteristic is an easily remembered simplicity. Perhaps the meaning 'by the way' gives us the clue. Proverbs are proverbially half-truths—against 'Many hands make light work' we can quote 'Too many cooks spoil the broth', and so on. They are true as far as they go, but they cannot (partly because of their brevity) cover the whole ground of truth even on the subject with which they profess to deal. An illustration of what is meant by this can be found in John 10^{6}. It is true that the relation of Jesus to His disciples *was* like that of a shepherd and his sheep in the days of His flesh; it *is to be* like that of a vine and its branches ($15^{1ff.}$). So the allegory of the Good Shepherd is a '*paroimia*', a provisional description, true and illuminating for the time being. That of the Vine is not called a '*paroimia*'. While the relation between them was that of the Leader and His followers, He could only talk to them in *obiter dicta*, and His explanations were of necessity incomplete; afterwards He would be free to speak to them without reserve of the Father ($16^{25f.}$), for He would be no longer *with* them—He would be *in* them. This interpretation is all the more attractive in that it accords well with the emphasis, so marked in the Fourth Gospel, on the contrast between the earthly and the heavenly, the movement from dependence on outward signs to the faith which believes without seeing. (See especially John 3^{12}, 20^{29}.)

For the Synoptic Gospels, on the other hand, Old Testament passages like Psalm 49^{4} and 78^{2} are vitally important, for the First evangelist quotes the latter in 13^{35}. In both passages the word 'parable' is synonymous with 'a dark saying'—Briggs has 'poem' in Psalm 78^{2} (modern verse, it may be noticed, has largely gone back to the oracular idea of poetry), 'parable' in Psalm 49^{7}; Knox, in his new translation, has 'Mine to overhear mysteries, and reveal, with a harp's music, things of deep import' in Psalm 49, and in Psalm 78: 'I declare to you my meaning under a figure; I will utter age-long riddles.' But it seems to be clear that the word 'parable' itself does not really mean 'a dark saying' in Matthew 13^{35}, but rather *a light on a dark subject*, some mystery so difficult to explain in intelligible speech that its truth can only be illustrated, not defined in logical terms. It should be noticed that Mark associates parables with 'mystery', the First evangelist with 'mysteries' and 'secrets' (Mark 4^{11}, Matthew 13^{35}). Here we come to a question about which the two evangelists appear to differ. Mark seems to imply that the parables *were* enigmatic sayings deliberately substituted by Jesus Himself for His first straightforward message, which was 'The Kingdom of God is here; repent and believe in the good news' (Mark 1^{15}), because He desired, for the time being at least, to discourage casual, shallow, or preoccupied hearers, and concentrate His attention upon the few who, though at first no better fitted to understand His message than others, at least loved and followed Him with a devotion which disappointment and perplexity could not seriously shake. It is possible to turn the keen edge of 'To those who are outside, all My teaching takes the form of parables, *that* they may stare and stare and never see My meaning, and listen and listen and never make out what I say, *lest*', etc., by making the correct observation that the Aramaic word translated 'that' has almost as many meanings as the word 'that' in English. Indeed, the First evangelist himself, using Mark at this point, alters 'that' to '*because*', and so changes the whole meaning of the quotation. So interpreted, the text cited from Isaiah 6$^{9f.}$ means that Jesus was using parables, not to *veil* the truth from the unthinking, but to *unveil* it. He is only compelled to employ such methods because the truth is so deep that it can only be expressed to simple minds in figurative language. Modern scholars point out that the Aramaic word in question, like the English word 'that', can be used as a relative pronoun, and translate '*who* stare and stare', etc.:[1] the text would then mean '*for* they', etc., and

[1] See T. W. Manson, *The Teaching of Jesus* (2nd Edition), pp. 74–80.

this is to all intents and purposes its meaning in the First Gospel.

All this may be true, but as we read the context our impression grows that the commentators are trying to save Mark from himself. Especially significant in this connexion is the fact that the First evangelist and Luke alike—both are following Mark at this point—have 'mysteries' where Mark has 'mystery' (compare Mark 4^{11} with Matthew 13^{11} and Luke 8^{10}). This cannot be a mere coincidence, nor can there be any question here of the First evangelist being dependent on Luke, or vice versa; we suspect that Mark is responsible for an alteration in the original tradition here, and that the other two evangelists, independently of each other, have corrected him. If so, the probability is that Mark is here under Pauline influence, and is thinking of Romans 11^{25}. This passage runs: 'For I would not have you ignorant, brethren, of this *mystery*, . . . that a partial hardening has befallen Israel, until the full complement of the Gentiles has come in.' Paul's argument is to the effect that the mass of the Jewish people had, in the providence of God, been allowed to remain outside the Church, because Gentiles would not, in any considerable numbers, enter into a society preponderately Jewish. The branches of the olive tree were broken off to leave room for others to be grafted in. This was 'contrary to nature', says Paul, as of course it is, as all experts in grafting know.

I suggest then, that Mark accepted this view, but carried the argument farther. If this was God's purpose, he argued, Jesus must have understood and accepted it, and therefore provoked the rank and file of the Jews to reject Him. However much so ruthless a policy must have pained Him, He regarded it as one ingredient in the bitter cup which He was to drink. The strange turn given—in Mark alone—to the saying about the lamp a few verses later on rather goes to confirm the theory that this was Mark's own belief: 'There is nothing hidden, except that it may be brought to light; nor did it become a *mystery*, but that it might come into the open.' Jesus, Mark believed, was hiding the truth in parables in order that it might make a more effective appearance later on, and—this is the most important point—to *a larger constituency*. This explanation of the reserve of Jesus may be right or wrong—we may well believe that Mark was mistaken—but it is obvious that there is a mystery here which cries out for explanation. The view that the motive for concealment was revelation at the appropriate time to the people who needed it most, though harsh, is not unworthy of an evangelist who was a much more thoughtful and penetrating student of the Gospel than has generally been supposed. On Good Friday—as Mark himself takes care to bring out—the 'veil of the Temple was rent in two from top to bottom' (15^{38}), and the lamp hidden in the secret place, the Holy of holies, became the light of the world. But our appreciative recognition of the fact that what we should call the missionary motive is the leading idea underlying Mark's treatment of his material should not prevent us from seeing that he has imposed an artificial pattern on a much simpler tradition. Its artificiality becomes clear in the explanation of the parable of the Sower given in Mark $4^{14ff.}$, almost universally regarded by modern commentators rather as a more or less official exposition added later than as containing authentic words of Jesus. In Mark $4^{33f.}$ we have an example of the later elaboration side by side with the simpler original—Saxon and Norman side by side, so to speak: 'And with many such parables He was speaking the word to them, *in so far as they were able to hear*, and without a parable He spoke not to them, while in private He was in the habit of explaining everything to His disciples.' 'As they were able to hear' surely implies that parables were, after all, used because the common people *could* make something of them, whereas in the reference to explanations reserved for the twelve, Mark is still insisting that, whatever they made of them, the real truth behind them was reserved for a more restricted audience. No wonder the Gnostic heretics, and (later on) ecclesiastical theology seized avidly upon these suggestions of secret doctrines imparted only to the twelve, whose successors and heirs were declared to be the bishops and clergy.

Though he retains Mark's somewhat stereotyped explanation, and appends another to the parable of the darnel in the wheat, the First evangelist's emphasis lies all the other way. We have seen that he corrects Mark $4^{10ff.}$; more significant still is the fact that *another* quotation from the Old Testament becomes the climax up to which the whole *parable-section* in his Gospel moves. It comes from Psalm 78^{2}: 'I will *open my mouth* in parables; I will *blurt out things kept secret* from the beginning.' I can find no phrase in modern English except 'blurt out' that does justice to the still more violent word in the original. When we read at the beginning of the Sermon on the Mount that Jesus 'opened His mouth', or in 2 Corinthians 6^{11}, 'My mouth is opened to you, Corinthians', we must undoubtedly interpret the meaning of the phrase to be 'to open one's heart'. The First evangelist, at least, is in no doubt as to whether our Lord did or did not take the common people into His confidence. He called, *not* a select group of disciples, but all 'the weary and heavy-laden' sons and daughters of His people to 'learn of' Him and so 'find rest for their souls' (Matthew 11^{28-9}). He will not break (and throw away as not fitted for His purpose) the crushed and battered reed, 'whereupon, if a man lean, it will go into his hand and pierce it' (Isaiah 36^{6}), or 'quench the wick of a smoking lamp' (Matthew 12^{20}); He will sow the seed over hill and dale, fruitful and unfruitful ground alike, until, when all His sowing does not suffice, on one barren hill He will sow Himself.[2] Here, surely, we must take our stand with the First evangelist; parables were designed not to veil, but to unveil, the truth. That does not alter the fact that they are not so simple as they appear at first sight; no merely casual hearer will see anything in them but more or less paradoxical sayings or more or less interesting stories. The warning, 'He that hath ears *to hear with*, let him hear', along with 'Take heed how you hear' is continually necessary.

To come to more modern definitions of 'parable': everyone is, of course, familiar with 'an earthly story with a heavenly meaning'. Our discussion of the subject so far might suggest that this definition is not so far wide of the mark as has sometimes been suggested; indeed, it might be regarded as a rough approximation to the truth, if it was not obvious that some of the gospel-parables contain no narrative at all. We may quote in this connexion Mark 3^{23} ('And summoning them (the scribes) He said to them *in parables*, How can Satan cast out Satan?', etc.), and Luke 6^{39} ('He spoke a *parable* to them, Can a blind man lead a blind man?', etc.). It will be noticed that both these 'parables' begin with a question—perhaps we ought to add Mark 4^{21}: 'Does the lamp come (into the room) to be put under an upturned pot or under the bed?', for it is introduced by the words 'And He said to them' in exactly the same way as the parables of the Sower and the seed growing secretly. The same observation applies to 'With

[2] A somewhat modified quotation from that great expositor of Scripture, the late Miss Lily Dougal.

what measure you mete, it shall be measured in return to you' (Mark $4^{24f.}$). Other examples can be found in Luke 14^{7} and perhaps 12^{41}. These parabolic sayings we must reserve for discussion in Chapter Two. Another somewhat frivolous definition ('A heavenly story with no earthly meaning') will not do either, though it shows an odd affinity with the Marcan idea discussed above, so long as it is interpreted as 'A heavenly story with no meaning that unspiritual people can understand'. Curiously enough, I came across what seems to be a better definition than either of these when reading—in the train—a book by that great humourist, Mr. P. G. Wodehouse. I am afraid that I must have given the book away, for I have never been able since then to verify the reference, and can only give its purport; it is not within my power to reproduce Mr. Wodehouse's nervous English. 'What do you call', says one of his characters, 'that "what-you-may-call-it" in the Bible that looks like a straightforward yarn when you begin to read it, but turns out to have something up its sleeve that pops out at you and leaves you flat before you've finished?' His friend answers: 'I suppose you mean a parable.' The essence of a parable is that it contains what I may call a 'bolt from the blue', whether the parable is in narrative form or consists of one or more paradoxical sayings.

If not all the parables in the Gospels are stories at all, it is also true that not all the stories in the Gospels are called parables. Neither the story of the Good Samaritan, nor the Prodigal Son, nor the Unjust Steward, nor Dives and Lazarus, nor the Friend at Midnight, nor the Lost Coin, nor—according to some early texts—the Pharisee and the Publican, is called by Luke a parable at all. I have sometimes thought that the reason for this—if it is not purely accidental—might be that Luke thought that brevity was essential to a parable; but the parable of the Sower is not so very short, and the Lost Coin and the Friend at Midnight cannot be called long. Perhaps light can be found on this question by comparing two short passages—both taken from Luke's Gospel and related to each other by a whole series of words common to both of them—one of which is called a parable, and the other is not. They are Luke 12^{37} (see verse 41) and $17^{7ff.}$. But the questions may be asked, 'May not the word "parable" [3] in verse 41 refer to the saying about the householder waiting up to catch the

[3] 'Lord, dost Thou say this *parable* to us?' etc.

burglar?' It is true that it intervenes between the passage about the master waiting upon his slave and Peter's question. But that great teacher, Professor Gwatkin of Cambridge, pointed out in my hearing long ago the fact that it is characteristic of Peter to refer back to a previously uttered saying of Jesus, ignoring intervening matter. When something his Master said set him thinking, he would for the moment become abstracted, and was only ready with his question a little while later.

Examples of this habit of Peter's can be found in several places. In Matthew 18[15] Jesus is reported as saying, 'If thy brother sin, go tell him his fault between thee and him alone', then going on to speak of Christian fellowship and prayer. Only in verse 21 does Peter come in with 'If my brother sin *against me*,[4] how often am I to forgive Him?' Again, in Matthew 19[16], the rich young ruler, as we call him, is described as coming to Jesus, and Jesus bids him leave all to follow Him; after he has gone, Jesus tells His disciples how sorry they should be for rich people, because they have so much to leave behind them when they enter the Kingdom. Peter, like other poor men, is not deeply moved by the contemplation of the troubles of the rich, and only intervenes six verses lower down with his habitual personal application: 'Lo! he says, *we* have left all to follow Thee; what about us?' Once more, in John 13[33], Jesus says, 'Whither I go, you cannot come', and in verse 36 Peter says: 'Where art Thou going, Lord?' Is it fantastic to suggest that in Luke 12[37-41] we have another instance of the same habit of mind, and that 'this parable' refers back to the saying about the master waiting upon his slave, four verses earlier? In any case, 'Who then is the trustworthy businesslike slave' in verse 42 has a much closer connexion with verse 37 than with verse 39 ('If the master of the house had known at what hour the burglar was coming', etc.), for the latter has to do, not with a faithful slave, but a sensible householder. Incidentally, still more poignancy is given to the passage if we accept the shorter reading of the 'Western' text in verse 41, and omit 'or even to all'. Then we get a fine example of the deep humility of Peter, which reappears in 'Depart from me, for I am a sinful man, Sir' (Luke 5[8]) and in 'Lord, dost *Thou* wash *my* feet' (John 13[6]), and perhaps in 'Rabbi, is it right for *us* to be here?' (a possible translation of

[4] The words 'against thee' are not found in the best texts of Matthew 18[15f.]; Peter, like the rest of us, invariably tends to apply general statements to personal issues.

Mark 9^{5}). So in Luke 12^{41} what Peter asks is: 'Dost Thou speak this parable to *us*, Lord? Do you mean that you will wait upon *us*?'[5]

If this interpretation of Luke $12^{37, 41}$ is accepted, it will be clear that the passage about the master waiting upon his slave is called a 'parable', the twin-passage about the slave waiting on his master (Luke $17^{7f.}$) is not. That they are contrasted with one another is obvious from the fact that they have so many words in common, such as 'pass along', 'gird oneself', 'wait upon', 'recline at table'. Luke $17^{7ff.}$ reads: 'Which of you who has a slave ploughing or shepherding, when he has come in from his work will say to him, *Pass along*, and *recline* at the table? Will he not rather say to him, Get ready my meal; *gird yourself* and *wait upon* me until I have dined and after that you shall eat and drink? Will he thank his slave because he obeyed his commands? So also with you; when you shall have done all that was commanded, you say, We are slaves:[6] we have only done our duty.'

It is interesting to notice that this is the only passage in the four Gospels in which we hear anything about doing our duty, but the chief reason why I have brought these two contrasted pictures of the relation between master and slave together is that the first (Luke 12^{37}) is described as a parable, and the second is not. As I have said, this might be regarded as an accident—we cannot press the argument from silence too hard—but at any rate the suggestion is worth making that the essence of the parable, whether it takes the form of a pronouncement—to use a technical term of form-criticism—or a narrative, is the element of surprise. When the tired slave waits upon his master we are concerned with the natural order of things; when the master waits upon the slave we are, on the other hand, in the realm of grace, in the 'Kingdom'. We are familiar with the great who think it an honour to their underlings to be allowed to wait upon them, but 'It is not so with you', says Jesus; 'whoever wants to become really great among you shall wait upon the others, and whoever wants to be first shall be your slave'.[7] The last thing Peter expects or indeed desires is that Jesus should wash his feet,

[5] The acted parable of the feet-washing in John 13 provides a striking parallel here.

[6] Omitting 'unprofitable' with our earliest version (the 'Lewis' Syriac). It is clearly out of place here, coming from a memory of the parable of the Talents (Matthew 25^{30}). Whether the slave is profitable or not, he has only done his duty.

[7] Mark 10^{45}.

but He does so all the same.[8] I hope to show in later chapters that the element of risk is native to the parable-story, side by side with that of surprise, and that this is why, for instance, the Lost Sheep is called a parable, and the Lost Coin is not, the Unjust Judge and the Widow is a parable and the Friend at Midnight is not. But this is to anticipate conclusions which can only be justified by detailed exposition of individual examples.

[8] John 13[6].

CHAPTER TWO

PARABOLIC SAYINGS

WE NOTICED in the course of the last chapter that some of the sayings called 'parables' in the Synoptic Gospels are led up to by a question—'How can Satan cast out Satan?' being one example. The question always expects, as the grammarians say, the answer 'No'. In 'How can Satan cast out Satan?', introduced as it is by 'He . . . said unto them in parables' (Mark 3[23]), Jesus would seem to have been dealing with two problems at the same time; one, How is it that respectable people like the scribes can bring themselves to utter such an infamous slander as 'He casts out demons by Beezeboul, prince of demons'?—this is dealt with in the rest of the paragraph—the other: Why is the prince of darkness apparently letting his victims go free without a struggle? In the words with which we are dealing Jesus passed from one question to the other. The suggestion that Satan can cast out Satan seems to imply either that the devil is playing some deep and crafty game of bluff, in other words, that he is allowing Jesus to achieve a little obvious success at the expense of the small fry of the demon-world in return for certain unspecified but important service in other directions, as football or boxing-matches are thought sometimes to have been squared beforehand; or, alternatively, that there is civil war in his kingdom. The first alternative is dismissed as involving absurd consequences; it implies that those of the Pharisee-party, who are themselves—and with some success—achieving exorcisms, are in the devil's pay too! The second has greater plausibility, for the same idea is involved in such proverbs as 'Set a thief to catch a thief' and 'When rogues fall out, honest men come into their own'. The real reason for the wholesale expulsion of the powers of darkness is, however, altogether different, and here comes in the real 'bolt from the blue'. Mr. Strongman is still strong, because his kingdom is still united, but he is just not quite strong enough, for Mr. Strongerman has come upon the scene and is taking a hand in the game: the devil is suffering from *force majeure!*

For one paradoxical explanation of an obvious fact—the mass-expulsion of demons—Jesus substitutes another, still more surprising to a generation which, like ours, had become so accustomed to seeing the devil get the best of it that thoughtful people had been forced to take refuge in eschatology as many modern theologians have recourse to Barthian theology. 'If I by the finger of God cast out the demons', says Jesus, 'you can see for yourselves that God is triumphantly at work: here, in this demon-haunted world is the evidence of His mastery of the situation in which you find yourselves.'[1]

The next parabolic saying—confining our attention to Mark's Gospel for a moment—is: 'Does a lamp come [into the room] to be put under an upturned corn-bin or a bed, not that it may be put on the lamp-stand?' Again, it is to be observed, the saying is introduced by a question expecting the answer 'No'.[2] The surprise comes in the words which follow: 'There is nothing hidden, except that it may be brought to light; nor was it a mystery, except that it might come into the open.' By smoothing out the question into a straightforward negative statement, the other Synoptic evangelists have blunted the keen edge of the paradox; it is true that things are sometimes hidden, but the purpose of secrecy is not love of mystery for its own sake, for 'God is light, and in Him is no darkness at all', but the fact that premature revelations may merely bewilder the minds of men whose minds are not ready yet to receive them. What is easily intelligible to the sixth form may be utterly meaningless to the lower fourth. To men accustomed to the idea of a God who dwells in thick darkness and, if He revealed Himself to men at all, keeps His secrets for 'his servants, the prophets' (Amos 3[7])—for the rank and file even of the chosen people the word was 'even if a beast touch the mountain, it shall be stoned'—the new and amazing truth is proclaimed that the vision of God was now open to all simple-minded people.[3]

We should observe in passing that 'He that hath ears to hear

[1] See Luke 11[20], Matthew 12[28].

[2] Replaced by a negative statement both in Luke 8[15] and Matthew 5[15] ('No one lights a lamp', etc.).

[3] Hebrews 12[18ff.] is a splendidly eloquent expression of this amazing truth; the very purpose of Sinai was to make the glory that was to follow more glorious still (2 Corinthians 3[10ff.]). See also for a confirmation of this idea, Matthew 11[25ff.] and Luke 10[22]. Here we pass from 'to simple-minded people also' to 'to simple minds and *not* to the wise and prudent'!

with, let him hear' is appended to Mark 4^{21} as it is to the parabolic narrative of the Sower and His seed (Mark 4^{9}). This surely confirms our view that the saying about the lighted lamp is thought of by the evangelist as the second of the parables of the Kingdom. We may compare with it 'Hear what the unjust judge saith' (Luke 18^{6}); both seem to be equivalent of our 'N.B.', and our Lord's 'Verily I say to you' (literally 'Amen': 'This is God's truth') which in the Fourth Gospel gains added solemnity from the twice-repeated 'Amen', making the saying an oath according to Rabbinic usage.[4] Such expressions are equivalent to our habit of calling attention to passages in a modern book by the use of italics.

The third parabolic saying in Mark (4^{24}) takes a different form. Not a question, but a generally accepted maxim introduces the pronouncement in this case; it is 'With what measure you mete, it will be measured in return to you', or 'You will be done by as you did'. The words 'And you will get a bonus in addition' transfer us from the realm of mathematics into that of grace. But the 'parable' (the bolt from the blue) comes in the words: 'For to him that has something already, shall receive more, and from him that has nothing, even what he has shall be taken away from him.'[5] That this saying appeared to involve unfairness is proved by Luke 19^{25}, which, even though it is probably not part of the original text, shows what the preacher or copyist who inserted it thought. As the principle is fully set forth in the parabolic story ('the pounds') to which we shall come in due course, no further exposition is necessary here. The other 'parables' in Mark 4 all contain narrative, and are to be studied in another chapter.

We turn then to Luke $6^{39f.}$, which also is introduced by a question, and is called a 'parable' by Luke. It runs: 'Can a blind man lead a blind man? Will not both fall into a ditch?' Again, the parable proper is to be looked for in the amazing statement which follows in 6^{40} ('Every disciple when he has been perfected shall be like his Teacher'). It goes without saying that when

[4] Strictly speaking the 'Yes, yes' 'No, no' of Matthew 5^{37} would be classed by the Rabbis as an oath. The meaning of the passage seems to be: 'If you must swear, don't go beyond the simple oath implied by a double "Yes" and "No".' 'Amen' should be understood as meaning not 'So be it', but 'So it is'.

[5] Again, Luke blunts the edge of this violent paradox by writing 'what he seems to have' or 'what he thinks he has' instead of 'what he has' (8^{18}). In 19^{26}, however, he leaves the original paradox untouched.

teacher and taught fall together into the ditch, they become equals in misfortune. In the 'parable' this ironical state of affairs is touched with a sudden glory, and transfigured. What happens sadly too often in the natural course of affairs is to happen gloriously in the kingdom of grace;[6] teacher and taught are to be one at last! Our next Lucan example ($14^{7,\ 11}$) is especially interesting, because the word 'parable' is used here of a surprising saying, and the narrative which begins at verse 16 is *not* called a parable; we should have labelled the story of the rich man's feast a parable without more ado, but no careful reader can fail to see that the 'parable' of Luke 14^{7} refers to the pronouncement of verse 11, to which all intervening matter leads up. By taking it for granted that 'He that humbles himself shall be exalted, etc.' transfers the subject under discussion to another world than this, commentators have been betrayed into imitating the pious gentleman who exclaimed, 'Blessed is he who shall be asked out to dinner in the Kingdom of God'; they forget that Jesus is talking of something as earthly as a dinner-party.

This is only one of many ways of escape from the sharp edge of a saying which common observation suggests is not only surprising, but demonstrably not true at least in this world the only world we know much about. The 'wisdom' of the earlier Jesus, the son of Sirach, is nearer to the facts, as most of us see them; it runs: 'If a mighty man invite thee, be retiring, and so much the more will he invite thee. Press not upon him, lest thou be thrust back, and stand not far off, lest thou be forgotten.'[7] Whether dignities, powers, and emoluments (which so often come to the man who contrives to be always among those present when such things are to be conferred) are really worth having may well be questioned: but that our Lord's pronouncement on this subject is *not* the principle by which such men rise to high official Church or State position cannot justly be denied. Here our Lord, as so often, flatly contradicts our values, and we are merely more or less adroitly evading the issue, when we have recourse to such plausible half-truths as the suggestion—which has been the subject of many a discourse—that Jesus said things with exaggerated emphasis in order to stamp them on His

[6] A similar idea can be found in Matthew 10^{25}, but there the equality lies in the realm of suffering rather than positive achievement.

[7] Ecclesiasticus $13^{9f.}$.

hearer's memory, or again that the truths He laid down were general principles, not to be applied without many modifications. We must follow their spirit, we are told, and must take care not to turn them into something they were never meant to be, a code of law. There is just enough truth in these warnings to lead us astray. It is true that our Lord did not give us a set of rules for daily living to be obeyed as we obey the laws of England, largely because we know that we shall suffer if we break them. But His words are *law*, all the same, in the Bible meaning of the word; that is, not so much a book of rules as a revelation of reality. It is so because He said so, and we have no business to explain His words away, because they do not square with our ideas of practical politics. His words do indeed deliberately and flatly contradict what most experienced men of affairs consider to be true. That is not because most men are rogues or fools, but because our world has always been managed in one way, while God works in another; this is one reason why both the Churches and the world in which they have to live are in their present distress; whatever we hear or say in church, the vast majority of well-meaning would-be Christians—not to mention able and well-disposed people outside the Churches—have come to assume that what God says is true, is not true in life as they know it. There can be no question that here we have a 'bolt from the blue'; we have made a smooth truism of a saying of Jesus which, when taken seriously, becomes either a soul-shaking truth or sentimental nonsense, a motto in a Christmas cracker or a bomb. There are indeed two ways of treating Jesus: one is to regard Him as a saint or an artist, and One who 'spoke as never man spoke', to gush over Him without any honest attempt to answer the question, 'But is what He said really *true?*' The other is to listen with exasperated annoyance, and say: 'All very fine, but it just is not true; look here and there: all our experience disproves it.' I think our Lord would prefer the second way, which at least takes Him to mean what He says. If we really believe that His teaching is concerned with some Utopia in the clouds, we ought to be honest enough to say so; anything is better than pretending to agree or agreeing with mental reservations, for that is the hypocrisy which He denounced so fiercely. We must escape from sentimental pretences, however disillusioning the experience may be; we may sing 'Jesus shall reign', and enjoy singing it, but the plain truth is that this world will not have this Man to rule over it, and one reason why so many thoughtful people do not think it worth their while to join the Churches is that they think—and with a certain amount of justification—that we are shouting to keep our courage up, that we have never really faced the facts either of life or of our Master's teaching. The issue is this: do we or do we not believe that when Jesus speaks, God speaks; that what He says is so because He said it, whatever our experience of Life suggests to the contrary? That means: Is the success that is gained by pushing ourselves forward, by discreetly canvassing for office or allowing our name to be brought forward with suitable testimonials, and so on (however roundabout and diplomatic our procedure may be) really worth achieving? Is not the whole business of 'making a name for oneself' in the Church a sham and a fraud, which would not impose upon us for a moment if we had not become so accustomed to it that we have come to take it for granted or dismiss it with a shrug of the shoulders? I have only dealt with this particular pronouncement at such length because it seems to me a striking example of the danger deadly to the soul of Christian honour, of taking what were meant to be and indeed are bombshells as high-sounding generalities.

If 'Everyone who exalts himself shall be humbled, and he who humbles himself shall be exalted' should be a 'bolt from the blue' to us, the next parable-pronouncement on our list was certainly a bombshell to those who first heard it. It is introduced by the parabolic formula, 'Hear me all of you, and understand' (Mark 7^{14}) and runs: 'There is nothing that enters into the man from outside that can defile him; only the things which *come out from inside the man* defile him.' Once again, the explanation of internal trouble universally given in those days is rejected, and a diagnosis to the last degree paradoxical substituted for it.[9] John Wesley told his preachers to 'tell everyone what you think of him to his face'; 'make haste', he said, 'to cast the fire out of your bosom'. Did he regard this liberty as merely the prerogative of the ministry? In any case, experience has taught most of us that his advice here is not to be taken too literally; there is often much to be said in favour of hiding one's light under a bushel. Does one really cast the fire out of one's bosom by casting it *into*

[9] It should be observed that Matthew 15^{15} expressly calls it a 'parable'.

someone else's? So-called righteous indignation is only too often camouflaged bad temper! But many psychologists would agree with Wesley that the sooner dangerous matter is evacuated the better for everybody concerned. But the question still remains: Does getting it off one's chest really deal with the trouble if the poison is still being produced within? In any case, here is another flat contradiction, not only of an idea common to all the religions of the ancient world, but much to the fore in the Old Testament itself. No wonder that the Pharisees were 'put off'—an admirable suggestion for the great New Testament word 'scandalized', made by Father Ronald Knox—by this veritable 'bolt from the blue'!

Of course, many more—if not most—of the sayings of Jesus might be dealt with in this way. Examples may be found in 'Love your enemies', 'He that saved his life shall lose it', and so on. They are all highly paradoxical, and imply the same reversal of accepted values. I have confined myself to those pronouncements which, either actually or by implication, are called 'parables', partly because the space allowed me makes it impossible for me to deal with all the 'Verilies' and 'Verily-Verilies' in such detail, and partly because my subject is not the teaching of Jesus generally, but 'parables' in the Gospels. These cases should be regarded merely as examples of a method of teaching native to the Synoptic Gospels, and therefore, almost certainly, to our Lord Himself.

CHAPTER THREE

GOD IN NATURE

IN THIS chapter we are to turn from parabolic pronouncements to parables which contain narrative, and deal first with those concerned chiefly with the surprising things to be seen in God's handiwork in what we call nature; in a later chapter we shall watch God at work in men's intercourse with one another. Strictly speaking, of course, we ought to speak of God at work in *man's* dealing with nature, for the human element always comes in. A human sower is seen going out to sow his seed, a man plants the seed which grows secretly in the ground, a man sows the mustard-seed, a woman puts the leaven in the meal. But the human action is not the pivot of the narrative in either case, and to emphasize it might lead us astray. I have not called these parables—of which the most obvious examples are the Sower, the Seed growing Secretly, the Mustard Seed, and the Leaven (though there are others)—'parables of the Kingdom' simply because I regard all the true parables of Jesus as equally parables of the Kingdom.

We have already emphasized the fact that 'He that hath ears to hear, let him hear', or some variant of that warning, is characteristic of the parable; now we have to add 'Look' to 'Hear'. 'Look! the sower goes out to sow,' He says. In every case Jesus is concerned with a cross-section of what we call 'nature', a word He could never have used, for to Him this world was alive with God, and wherever His Father was at work, there was nothing that was not supernatural in the sense that we may know that it happened, but *how* it happened no one can tell us. But we shall not really 'see' the Kingdom of God in these everyday miracles of nature and human life unless we look and look again, and not only look, but mark the spot at which the vision came to us, that we may know where it will repay us to make further explorations. It is not enough to 'stand and stare', for though in certain moods we are easily impressed, we soon forget. And if we exploit our discoveries to make conversation, if we are content to tell a friend what we have seen, and pass on, or put it away in some commonplace book in our memory to be used as a striking illustration in our next religious address, we are not receiving the Kingdom of God 'as a little child', and cannot enter into it.

This is the besetting sin of the preacher. We might emend Isaac Watts and read: 'Whene'er I take my walks abroad how many do I see—children's addresses in the sod, and sermons in the tree.' The question for all of us is: What is our real treasure, and where do we keep it? Is it our reputation as preachers, the success of the causes we favour most, or is it the realization, not merely as a doctrine to be expounded to others with power and effect, but as the truth which made the incarnation possible, of the fact that 'God is with us', here in this fallen world. Long after the twelve had been told that it was theirs to 'know the mysteries of the Kingdom of God', Jesus still had to tell them that they could not yet use their eyes and ears (Mark 4^{11}, 8^{18}). Looking for some sensational manifestation of the glory of God, they were for ever thinking of the next item on their planned agenda, and could not see what was going on under their eyes. 'We thought', they said, 'that it was He who would redeem Israel'; 'Lord, dost thou at this time restore the kingdom to Israel?'; 'Lord, show us the Father: that is all we want'—and His answer was always: 'Have I been so long with you, and have you not *seen?*'

It was not only His enemies who asked for a 'sign from Heaven' —we are all for ever doing the same thing. If He were with us in the same way as He was with them, surely one of the first things He would do would be to recall us from our unending and often unprofitable discussions of the question, What are the Churches to do next? and say: 'Look what God *is* doing!' But we must carry our Lord's burning-glass about with us, if we are to see for ourselves 'every common bush afire with God', and what is more important—'why the bush is not consumed'.[1]

The parable of the Sower has been called a 'parable on parables'. Its point of overwhelming surprise is the fact that, though most of the seed sown admittedly comes to little or nothing, the little that falls into good ground yields miraculously abundant results, and does so because the life of God is in it. The explanation which follows in all three Synoptic Gospels is

[1] Exodus 3^{3}.

somewhat misleading, because it turns the parable into an allegory, that is, it makes of a description of observed fact a theme for moralization, a vision into a sermon. But it does bring into relief a problem which in the preacher's and teacher's life becomes more burdensome as the years go by; it is what is the use of all this talking, of the expense of nerve and spirit in a waste of half-attention or—as seems to happen only too often—genial indifference? 'Full many a flower is born to blush unseen and waste its sweetness on the desert air'—this observation is at least as true of our gems of eloquence and flowers of speech. And—a far more important matter—what of the wasted good in the world? The answer is God does not seem to worry too much about it, and neither should we. The Father sends His rain and sunshine down on the evil and the good, and simply goes on being God, giving Himself, however unthankful and churlish the recipients of His bounties show themselves to be. Here, at least, natural and revealed religion speak with the same voice, for they both show us a God apparently both unthrifty and undiscriminating. The problem of wasted good becomes appalling when we think of the fresh young life poured into this world to become food for powder or the atomic bomb, or—more tragically still—ruined by its heredity or environment almost before it has time to be born. But the fact remains that it is so, and all our necessary insistence on the 'wrath of God' should never be allowed for an instant to blind us to the free, forgiving love which pours like sunshine and life-giving rain on this—in the literal sense of the word—*hateful* world of ours. All the same, just because the seed which He is for ever sowing is Himself, the little that does not seem to be utterly wasted yields so great a harvest that all the disappointment and heartbreak may be at any moment swallowed up in glory and joy. This is the abiding miracle—that there *is* good ground still, in spite of all the weeds and stones, and that *it is still so good.* That this is true in nature we take for granted, miraculous as it is, though we are apt to be sceptical when we hear of miracles of grace. We assume as a matter of course that 'while the earth endures, seed-time and harvest, summer and winter, shall not cease', and at the same time are more than half-inclined to despair of the Church of God.

The parable of the Sower has sometimes been interpreted as though Jesus was in a somewhat pessimistic mood when He uttered it, and indeed the explanation which follows it, with its detailed description of hindrances to the growth of the seed, gives it that appearance, as though our Lord was finding His popularity a burden and was beginning to doubt the use of talking.[2] It might indeed be prefaced by the headline 'Facing the facts', but if we look a little deeper into the context of these early parables of Jesus, we shall see that their general subject might be summarized as follows: in spite of obvious difficulties, such as (1) the admitted fact that a large proportion of God's best gifts and man's sacrificial labours are wasted or misused, the harvest will come; (2) the fact that human nature—the soil—is, in many respects, diseased, the earth is still capable *of itself* of bringing forth fruit; (3) the fact that evil seed also is being sown in the field of the world, and again and again seems to be strangling the good, it is still safe to leave both to grow together; (4) the fact that the seed sown is the smallest and least conspicuous of all seeds, it has properties which are to cover the earth. Each parable in turn states a problem which is faced squarely, and answers it with the same confidence in the divine and therefore unconquerable power contained in the good seed which is the Gospel of the Kingdom.

We pass on, then, to the parable of the Seed growing Secretly (Mark 4[26ff.]). Here all that is necessary is that the seed should be sown, and that it should be the right seed; the soil on the one hand with its God-implanted properties—the rain, the sunshine, and the process of the seasons—can be trusted to do the rest. The corn grows to ripeness, while the farmer goes about his other business, and he can sleep securely knowing that the harvest will not fail. Indeed, the harvest comes so quickly that it is often ready for cutting before he is prepared for it. The 'surprise' here surely is to be found in the fact that even our perverted human nature in a fallen world is capable still of bearing fruit *of itself*.

When I read the fulminations of some Barthians about human nature and its complete alienation from God, I am almost persuaded, but then I come back to the Gospels and find them alive with faith in as yet unregenerate men and women. Did not our generous Master tell His bitterest foes that the Kingdom of God

[2] Perhaps Jesus did sometimes feel this, as we all do. 'Why do I talk to you at all?', He said once, if one possible translation of John 8[25] is accepted. If so, that only shows once more that He was 'tempted at all points as we are'.

was 'within them'?[3] What seems to be clear is that we trust both the power of the Word and the capacity for response in the hearts and minds of men too little, and that we allow ourselves to be too easily disillusioned. Perhaps indeed the words 'sleep and wake night and day' suggest that we worry too much about the progress of the work of God, for plants do not thrive when they are always being uprooted and examined to see how they are getting on. If the parable of the Sower suggests that quickly visible results are often disappointing—most of us know that by painful experience—the seed growing secretly clearly implies that results *not* quickly visible are certain, if the *right* seed had been faithfully sown. Both these parables are focused round the 'harvest', but it will be convenient to delay our examination of the meaning of an idea which is common to all the parables discussed in this chapter to the end.

In the parable of the Mustard-seed (Mark $4^{30ff.}$=Matthew $13^{31f.}$=Luke $13^{18f.}$) Jesus goes on to say that the seed of the gospel is of such pungent and penetrating quality that in a comparatively short time it will grow into a tree which will overshadow the earth, and the birds (which T. W. Manson and others identify with the Gentiles) will nest in its branches. Not one of the parables has been more obviously and completely fulfilled than this. Western Christendom has grown up under the shadow of a Church which began as an incredibly inconspicuous movement. The history of the Western world has only once been changed right round, as the dating of our years proves. Roman imperialism, Greek philosophy, even Jewish nationalism, might have done it; they—to use the language of the parable—were 'seeds sown on the earth' (Mark 4^{31}), but each in its turn had to give way before this movement which began so unobtrusively, that for centuries, as a survey of contemporary non-Christian literature proves, the great world knew little or nothing about it, and what little was known it completely misunderstood. There was no mass-propaganda, no upsurging revolutionary movement behind it; only a Galilean peasant gathering round Him a group

[3] Luke 17^{21}. I am, of course, aware that some commentators translate 'in the midst of you', following the lead of the Old Syriac version. 'It is undoubtedly awkward', writes Creed, 'that the saying is addressed to the Pharisees, if it means "within"—as it usually does—but this objection is not decisive, for the meaning might be "in the hearts of men".' But surely it is only awkward for very bigoted people to admit that God might be at work in the heart of a Pharisee!

of young men, of whom only two or three have left any name behind them even in the history of the Church. He was crucified after a year or two, and *they* forsook Him; and Christendom came from that! Indeed, 'God has chosen the weak things of the world to confound the strong'; no historian before Christ could possibly have foreseen so mighty an effect from so insignificant a cause, and no historian since has ever been able to explain it; Gibbon's 'five causes' are ludicrously inadequate, in spite of the extraordinary skill with which they are set forth.

The parable of the Leaven (Matthew 13^{33}=Luke $13^{20f.}$) has given rise to some controversy. It has been pointed out that everywhere else in the New Testament 'leaven' symbolizes evil, Mark 8^{15}=Matthew 16^{6}=Luke 12^{1} and 1 Corinthians $5^{7f.}$ being quoted as examples. The truth seems to be that 'leaven' had become simply a synonym for bread among Jews at the beginning of the Christian era, as it is in Rabbinic Hebrew except in theology, in which the evil 'leaven' was spoken of in somewhat the same way as we speak of 'original sin'. 'Beware of the leaven of the Pharisees and the leaven of Herod' means 'Beware of intimate association with the Pharisees and Herod's people': it is to be compared with the condemnation of Jesus for His eating with publicans and sinners. At Passover-time, of course, leaven —a name used for the fragments of dough left on the sides of the pot from the last baking, which had undergone fermentation from exposure to the air and helped to 'raise' the next batch of bread —was evil, simply because it was matter in the wrong place; normally, leavened bread was regarded as in every way superior to unleavened bread. Indeed, even when used in its theological sense, the leaven was not evil in itself. God, it was said, implanted in the heart of man a 'leaven', a fermenting restlessness which prevented him vegetating like the cattle, and was the cause of progress and civilization. Sometimes it seems to have been identified with the sex instinct, but generally it was interpreted in a more comprehensive way, corresponding roughly to what psychologists call '*libido*'. In other words, it was morally neutral, capable of being either sublimated or exploited for base uses. With the fall of man it fell too, and became the mother of selfish ambition, jealousy, envy, and lust. The doctrine of a compensating good leaven (which we should call 'prevenient grace') appears to have been a later development. The idea then underlying the parable of the Leaven is that of a bubbling, fermenting, explosive force which decomposes only to recompose. As a matter of historical fact, the history of Christianity in the world has not been characterized by gradual and steady evolution, but by a series of crises. As Harnack said: 'The spirit of Paul has worked as a fermenting influence throughout the history of Christendom, and forgotten or ignored by the original Church for centuries, has broken out in explosion after explosion.' But this miraculous, because unaccountable, increase confronts us with another problem: What about the opposition, the kingdom of Satan? Whence comes the darnel in the wheat? I suppose that the parable of the darnel in the wheat (Matthew $13^{24ff.}$) may, like the others, be taken from actual life; a farmer might be spiteful enough to sow darnel in his neighbour's field, as it was true that the scribes from Jerusalem were sufficiently malicious to declare that Jesus cast out demons by the help of the ruler of all demons. The stupidity of this accusation was only equalled by the malice which lay behind it, and the disciples would only be too eager to execute summary vengeance, if they could, on the men who were guilty of so poisonous a slander. Jesus answers with the serene assurance of triumphant faith which rings out in 'With God nothing is impossible'. 'No', He says, 'you are not to root out the weeds to save the wheat; let both grow together; time will show.' It is true that, while men sleep and wake night and day, and time moves on to the inevitable consummation, evil as well as good seed is for ever growing secretly; a disturbing and very dangerous poison is everywhere at work in the field of divine activity. All the same, the good seed is indestructible; as 'while the earth endures summer and winter, seed-time and harvest shall not cease', so while the earth endures, the Kingdom of God shall not cease to prevail over the wickedness and folly of the devil and man. In the parable of the darnel and the wheat, the surprising element —the real 'parable'—is the fact that it is safe to let the weeds grow.

Dr. T. W. Manson writes that the idea that the farmer's men should wish to destroy the darnel to leave room for the wheat to grow is 'absurd', and 'cannot have been made in real life'.[4] Surely it is imaginable that farm-hands might make a foolish suggestion! He writes again: 'The reapers are not identical with

[4] *The Sayings of Jesus*, p. 193.

the farm-workers, but are apparently special workers employed for the harvest.' But, 'Again,' he argues, 'this does not square with real life. The farmer may employ extra men in harvest-time, but the regular workers also do their share.' I have the highest possible respect for Dr. Manson's powers of exposition, and have learned very much from him, but I confess that this seems to be hypercritical. 'I will say to the reapers' does not *necessarily* imply that they were a different body of men, and the reference to 'the angels' occurs only in the explanation which follows the parable (verses 37ff.), nor can I see why, if we regard the explanation which follows the parable of the Sower as secondary without impugning the authenticity of the parable itself, we should not mete out the same treatment to the parable of the darnel in the wheat. The point is important, because it affects our whole conception of what a genuine parable is, and what it is not. I agree that the stories Jesus told were not fictions invented to illustrate spiritual truth or teach moral lessons, like Aesop's fables; but Jesus did not tell stories even about life as He saw it merely because He enjoyed describing nature or human behaviour; He told them because He saw them to be relevant to the needs of His followers. The surprise expressed by the farmer when he found the darnel among the wheat suggests that it was an unusual phenomenon to find the two growing together—that they are very much alike, and produce similar grain (though darnel is slightly darker in colour) is well known.

The fact that this parable is so directly relevant to a definite crisis in the life of our Lord seems to me additional evidence for its authenticity. As I have already noticed, the hot-headed young followers of Jesus could hardly have heard of the slander about Beezeboul without itching to lay hands on the slanderers. In any case, no parable in the Gospels is more directly relevant to the history of the Church through the centuries. Serious attention to its obvious meaning would have made the martyrdom of alleged heretics impossible. Whether we should go farther, and say that the parable settles for believers the vexed question of capital punishment is perhaps doubtful, though the principle which is implicit in it—that it is futile to seek to bring about the extirpation of evil by putting men who have identified themselves with it, to death—may well lead us to doubt the efficacy of the death-sentence. But the case here is not unlike that involved in our

Lord's condemnation of divorce; believers may well regard both divorce and the killing of wrong-doers by judicial action as forbidden *to them*, and at the same time refrain, as He did, from seeking to force a community not yet content of its own volition to accept His principles as statutory law. That the parable itself has pacifist implications I am sure, and I have continually been surprised that pacifists of my acquaintance make apparently so little use of its aid in their arguments. But all our discussions on these subjects should not blind us to the fact that its *central* idea is the amazing truth that the good seed *can* survive at all in a world in which, by all reasonable human calculations, it should have been choked to death long ago. So hard to keep alive is the spark of grace, so ruthless, so interminably reproductive and contagious is evil, that even the final goal—i.e. the Kingdom of God come with power—often looks impossible of achievement. Yet with God all things must be possible—except conversion by force.

If, however, we pass from the realm of statutory law or international relations to that of Christian social philosophy, it seems to be clear that Christians who take this parable seriously—as Bishop Barnes seems reluctant to do—can make no compromise whatever with any theory of eugenics which would sterilize vicious stocks to prevent infection. That there is something radically wrong with even the most Christian-sounding versions of such theories is perhaps proved by the fact that, if any advocate of such drastic methods of dealing with an admittedly tragic situation took the trouble to go back far enough in his own family-tree, he would certainly come to a stage at which the only surviving representatives of his family would have been eradicated had a eugenist come along with the power to rid society of the mischief they were causing or likely to cause; and in that case where would the would-be reformer himself have been? These people leave out of account two things: one great, the other greater. One is the almost inexhaustible power of recovery in human nature; the other the regenerating power of the grace of God, which avails not only to redeem the individual, but the family. Of course, all parables from nature are to some extent misleading, for men and women can never be wheat or darnel; perhaps that is why Jesus passed so soon from parables from nature to parables chiefly concerned with people.

As I pointed out in *Jesus as They Saw Him*, sayings and parables of Jesus generally arrange themselves in pairs, which I then called 'antiphonal paradoxes'. The parable of the darnel in the wheat might correspond to that of the seed growing secretly, for good and bad seed alike are sown while men sleep, or alternatively, to that of the drag-net (Matthew 13[47f.]). The outstanding difference between the parable of the drag-net and the darnel in the wheat consists in the fact that in the former the fishermen get rid of the unsaleable fish at once; in the latter the farmer's men are *forbidden* to get rid of the darnel till harvest-time. The refrain appended to them both (verses 41f., 49f.) certainly seems to be out of place in the case of the drag-net. But this difficulty will have to be faced when we come to the discussion of the meaning of the phrase 'the harvest' or 'the consummation of the age', so common in the First Gospel. At this point we need only remark that after every miraculous draught of fish there must follow the separation of the bad fish from the good; sometimes indeed the weight of the catch is too heavy for the net, for human organization cannot cope with divine plenty (Luke 5[6]). The amazing thing here is that all sorts of people are to be drawn into the sphere of the Gospel's influence (cf. John 12[32]). 'Their fish shall be after their kinds, the fish of the great sea, exceeding many.'[5] Jesus told His first disciples that they were to be 'fishers of men', and fishing for men is always a risky business, whether we use the drag-net of an evangelistic mission, or the hook-and-line of private conversation. In that shocking and delightful book, *The Thousand and One Nights*, the reading of which has been too much neglected by students of the Gospels, the fisherman sometimes opens a fish's mouth to find a ring or jewel for which a great reward has been offered, but more often a monster leaps out and threatens to tear the fisherman to pieces, unless he is lucky enough to know the monster's name. Jesus himself was a past-master in the art of fishing for men, and told Peter once (Matthew 17[27]) that he was to 'take the first fish that comes up', the first man or woman who came along, and 'open his mouth'. When we read at the beginning of the Sermon on the Mount that Jesus 'opened His mouth', the reference is not to the excellence of His articulation—as I once heard an elocution lecturer at a theological college say—but that He took His disciples into His confidence. The fisherman must gain the confidence of—his victim, I was

[5] Ezekiel 47[10]

going to write, but victim is not perhaps the best word, for it suggests the 'confidence trick'—and, sooner or later, if he can get him to talk, and has himself the grace to listen, he will find what he is seeking, the image of God, the superscription of the king. He will discover that he, too, is current coin of the Kingdom of Heaven. I hope to return to this theme in Chapter Nine. It is noteworthy that *only the demon-possessed* are told to be quiet when they want to *talk to Jesus*. An American revivalist once preached a sermon on 'Behold, a sower went *forth* to sow', the preacher's point being that he did not put an advertisement in the local paper announcing that the Rev. Mr. So-and-So would preach at 11 and 6.30 the next Lord's day, and saying in effect, 'Now, all you land, come and be planted'! Jesus never waited for people to come and hear Him; apparently He preferred small to large congregations, and personal interviews to both. John the Baptist preached *at* people, and they flocked to listen as people will, if the preacher is denunciatory enough; they did not seem to mind being called or hearing other people being called 'vipers' brood'. As another American has truly said: 'If the Baptist had known about the five men that the Samaritan woman had been living with, he would have mentioned them to her in his first sentence. Jesus began the conversation by asking her for a drink, and only then told her all that ever she did.' But fishing is a risky business; you never know your luck, and this is specially true when you are fishing for men.

When Andrew went out fishing
All night on Galilee,
Full many a catch he made there,
A hundred fish or three;
''Tis just as the sea will have it;
Fisherman's luck', said he;
And then he went out fishing
For wilder fish than of yore,
And many a straining netfull
He dragged in to the shore,
And so on a cross they laid him,
'Fisherman's luck' once more.[6]

[6] A poem sent in for a prize offered in the *Saturday Westminster*, which I have taken the liberty of altering slightly.

From our lingering by the way, like the disciples, to pluck the ears of corn which hang temptingly over the path of our discourse, we turn to the consideration of the word 'harvest' which forms part of the refrain appended, in one form or another, to all the parables considered so far. It is also called 'the consummation of the age', but does 'the age' mean 'this period' or 'this world's history'? There can be little doubt, I think, that in the First Gospel at least, the phrase is taken as referring to a future consummation. 'Lo! I am with you all the days to the consummation of the age', the last words of this Gospel, seem to settle this.[7] Sayings, on the other hand, like 'Pray ye the Lord of the harvest, that He may send forth more labourers into His harvest' (Matthew 9^{38}=Luke 10^{2}) and 'The fields are already white to the harvest' clearly imply that the harvest has come already. On the whole, it seems probable that Jesus regarded the harvest as already come when He announced that 'the Kingdom of God is here' (see also 'If I by the finger of God cast out demons, then here is the Kingdom of God at your service'). But the fact that He regarded the decisive hour in the world's history as having already begun need not have prevented him foreseeing a future consummation. What seems to have happened here, as in Mark 13, is that the Synoptic evangelists did not see clearly a distinction, present to the mind of Jesus, between the 'harvest' or 'consummation of this age' and the consummation of the last age of the world's history. If so, the refrain, 'So shall it be at the consummation of the age', becomes part of the Church's explanation (as indeed it is in Matthew 13^{40}), not of the original parable.

We have two more parables of nature to deal with, both of which are concerned with the fig-tree. Is the 'parable' of the fig-tree spared a year longer really a 'parable' at all (Luke $13^{6ff.}$) in the sense in which we are using the word? It seems to stand on the border-line between parable and allegory; by this I mean that, like the story of the wicked husbandmen (Mark $12^{1ff.}$ and parallels), it bears the appearance of a story made up to illustrate a particular truth rather than an observation of what we call natural processes, or of the behaviour of ordinary men and women in actual life, both interpreted as revealing the supernatural in the natural. In this case, the truth to be illustrated is the transition of the Kingdom from Judaism to Christianity resulting

[7] Matthew 28^{20}.

from our Lord's last appeal to Jerusalem; but only when we read *four* sayings about the fig-tree together do we see its parabolic significance.

We will take the simplest first. It is—in Mark's version—'Now from the fig-tree learn its parable: when its branch becomes soft, and the leaves spring forth, you know that the summer is near; so also must you, when you see these things happening, know that He (the Son of Man) is near, even at the doors' ($13^{28f.}$). Here once more we are reminded of the miracles constantly taking place in what we miscall 'nature'. When men are aware only that 'as the days lengthen, the cold strengthens' and their 'hearts are failing them for fear of what is coming upon the world', precisely then, if they had learned their lesson from the coming of every day ('the darkest hour comes before the dawn') and every year ('the worst of winter ushers in the spring') they would lift up their heads, for look! the sap is moving in the trees, the Kingdom is here, waiting to meet men when they open their eyes and their doors, 'You know how to discern the signs of earth and sky; how is it that you cannot understand the times you live in?' (Luke 12^{56}).

It is significant that Mark appends to the second of our fig-tree passages (the so-called cursing of the barren fig-tree in $11^{12ff., 20ff.}$) a saying about the faith which moves mountains. This leads me to suggest that, in his version of this saying (Luke 17^{6}), it is *Luke* who gives us the clue to the whole series of fig-tree sayings. At first reading, 'If you have faith as a grain of mustard-seed, you shall say to this sycamine tree' (the black mulberry, thought of in Palestine as a kind of fig) ' "Be thou uprooted and planted in the sea" ' presents us with what looks like an insoluble enigma; how has the 'mountain' of Mark 11^{23}=Matthew 21^{21} (Mark) and Matthew 17^{20} ('Q')[8] become any kind of a fig-tree in Luke? And what is the use of uprooting fig-trees and planting them in the sea anyhow? It might seem as though Luke, who is generally believed to have been following 'Q' in this passage, remembered that in Mark the saying about moving mountains was connected with the cursing of the fig-tree, and got the mountain and the fig-tree somehow confused in his mind! But that does not account for 'planted in the sea', which suggests that the

[8] One of the comparatively few sayings of Jesus confirmed by Paul (1 Corinthians 13^{2}).

evangelist had heard a different version of the saying about faith as a grain of mustard-seed. In that case Luke 17^{6} should be assigned to 'L' (Luke's own collection of sayings and stories of Jesus), not to 'Q', the name given by scholars to the sayings of the Lord which are common to Luke and the First evangelist. The form of Luke 17^{6} need not be due then to a mere confusion.

To see what this involves we must go back for a moment to Mark $11^{21ff.}$. After 'have faith in God' comes the saying about the faith which moves mountains, and after that, first a saying about believing prayer, and then another concerning the necessity that such prayer should be accompanied by forgiveness of offenders (verse 25). The sequence of thought appears to be something like this: Jerusalem is at once the barren fig-tree and the great mountain-barrier which, instead of being a help to the evangelization of the world, had become its chief hindrance. It can be removed, like all other hindrances to the work of God, by faith in God expressing itself in human prayer. But behind this prayer, if it is to be effective, there must not lie hidden any lingering hatred of their Jewish persecutors; no personal resentment must lurk behind their requests for the removal of the barrier.

Luke 17^{6} takes the matter a step farther; the fig-tree of Judaism would never bear fruit in its native soil again,[9] but it was *not* dead. 'There is hope of a tree, if it is cut down; . . . through *the scent of water* it will bud, and put forth boughs like a plant' (Job $14^{7ff.}$). Transported into the great sea of the Gentile world, Israel was to come to vigorous life in the Church. There is an interesting parallel and contrast in the story of Ahikar, an Eastern household tale which was certainly familiar to Jesus, for He quotes it in Matthew $24^{48ff.}$=Luke $12^{45ff.}$. It runs, 'And Ahikar said to him (Nadab or Naidan): "O my boy! Thou art like the tree which was fruitless beside the water, and its master was fain to cut it down, and it said to him, '*Remove me to another place*, and if I bear not fruit, cut me down.' And its master said to it, 'Thou hast not borne fruit beside the water, how shalt thou bear fruit in another place?' ".'[10]

[9] Perhaps 'never' is too strong in view of developments during the last few months.

[10] This is according to the Arabic version: the Syriac version reminds us of Luke $13^{6ff.}$. It runs: 'My son, thou hast been to me like that palm-tree that stood by a river, and when its lord came to cut it down, it said to him, "Let me alone this year also, and I will bring thee forth carobs". And the master said to it, "Thou hast

So interpreted, the parable of Luke $13^{6ff.}$—which may, of course, be a story taken from real life—takes its appropriate place in the sequence. Jesus hopes for Jerusalem in Luke $13^{1ff.}$, He despairs of it in Mark 11^{14}, and hope springs out of despair in Luke 17^{6}. That the fig-tree and the vine are symbols of home-life in Palestine is shown by the proverbial phrase, 'Every man shall dwell under his own vine and his own fig-tree'; we should say 'under his own roof-tree', as the Arab would say 'under his palm-tree'. I have often wondered whether this is not the clue to the somewhat cryptic reference to the fig-tree in John 1^{48} ('Before Philip called you, when you were yet under the fig-tree, I recognized you'; or as we might say colloquially, 'I had my eye on you'). When we remember that Cana is the next village but one to Nazareth, may the words not mean simply: 'When you were still a boy at home'?

not been industrious in what is thine own, wilt thou be industrious in what is not thine own?".' It will be observed that Jesus turns this the other way round in Luke 16^{12}. It is significant, too, that the tree pleads for itself in Ahikar: in the Gospel the vine-dresser pleads for it: there is a world of difference here.

CHAPTER FOUR

PARABLES OF MEN AND WOMEN IN LUKE'S GOSPEL

WHEN WE pass from what we have called 'parables of nature' to those concerned chiefly with human life and behaviour, the abundance of material at our disposal compels us to devise some kind of order of treatment. Perhaps the best arrangement is to take first those narratives which Luke calls 'parables', and then the narratives in the First Gospel which begin with some such phrase as 'The Kingdom of Heaven is' (or 'shall be') 'likened to'—this may be regarded as the Matthean equivalent of the Lucan 'Another parable He put before them'. After that we will bring together those longer stories in Luke's Gospel *not* called 'parables'—some of which, however, show many of the characteristics of the authentic Gospel-parable. After that it will be necessary to make a collection of what we might call parabolic material; references to human life and behaviour introduced by such phrases as 'Is there a man amongst you?' or 'What man among you?' and so on. Finally, I hope to deal with two border-line cases in the First Gospel along with related material found here and there in Luke; in these, by the introduction of subject-matter drawn from another world than this, either what starts as a parable ends in allegory, or the whole story is allegorical from beginning to end.

Parables proper—that is, narratives called 'parables' by Luke —we have to deal with in this chapter are the slave whom the master waits on (but not the slave who waits on his master), the Lost Sheep (but not the Lost Coin), the Rich Fool, the Pharisee and the Publican (here, however, the word 'parable' is textually questionable, so I reserve its consideration for a later chapter), the Unjust Judge and the Importunate Widow (but not the Friend at Midnight), the Wicked Husbandmen (this, of course, is not peculiar to Luke), and the pounds entrusted to ten slaves.

Apart from the story of the Wicked Husbandmen, the only one of these narratives as to which there can be any reasonable doubt whether it is taken from actual human life, is that of the master waiting on his slave; it seems more natural to regard it as a description of our Lord's own attitude to His followers than, like the others, as a record of observation and experience. For it is not easy, to say the least of it, to imagine any master but Jesus going out of his way to get his slave's supper ready and wait upon him. In other words, we are here in the realm of grace rather than normal human relations. About the shepherd and his lost sheep there can be little question. This is what we can readily imagine an Eastern shepherd doing, but it is none the less a revelation of God at work in the minds and hearts of men in the world as we know it, and is therefore, in the strict sense, supernatural. Jesus not only focuses our attention upon miracles which we can see if we care to look, on every hand in the world of nature as God made it—He loves even more to take some scene from workaday life and the behaviour of ordinary people, and say: 'Look with all your eyes, for here also you can see God at work, and more surprisingly, for nature must obey her Creator, whereas men and women need not do so; *they* sometimes act like God, without compulsion'! There may have been no special risk involved in the shepherd searching for his lost sheep, but to leave the other ninety-nine 'in the wilderness' (Luke) or 'on the hills' (Matthew) to fend for themselves while he did so means that he runs the risk of losing some of them at least! It is important to notice that we are not told that they were left in the fold; the nearest shelter was perhaps far away, and there was no time to be lost. To leave them meant risking their safety, for there might well be wolves or human thieves about. Worldly wisdom tells us 'a bird in the hand is worth two in the bush', and it is as though Jesus answered: 'Yes, I know; but I know too that many a shepherd will risk ninety-nine sheep in his hand for one in the bush.' Ordinary men constantly exchange all their securities for adventures in which, even if they succeed, they can hope for little or no profit except the consciousness of achievement.[1]

[1] This parable, as it is reproduced in the First Gospel (Matthew 18[12ff.]), brings out this point even more impressively. Here the 'lost' sheep becomes a 'wandering' sheep, the difference implied being that, while the 'lost' sheep might have been lost by mere mischance, the 'wandering' sheep was in the habit of straying. It is what we might call 'the black sheep of the family' which is 'for ever wandering' (verse 12), the other sheep 'never having been known to go astray' (this is the exact meaning of the tense of the Greek verb in this passage). Our obstinate affection for the odd-one-out who will not fit into our arrangements may be, from any common-sense point of view, unjustifiable, and we label it one of the unaccountable kinks in human nature; being unaccountable, it is miraculous in the proper sense of that much-abused word, and is, says Jesus, one of the links that still binds us to God (Mark 2[17]).

It is clear that the element of risk as well as that of surprise must be regarded as one of the marks of the Gospel-parable. The Sower risked his precious seed on stony, shallow, and weed-infested soil; one farmer left doubtful soil and uncertain weather to do his work for him; another took the greater risk of allowing wheat and darnel to grow together to the harvest; and so on.

Where the element of risk is not perceptible, there is no 'parable'. What a risk was taken by the master who waited on his slave! (Luke 12^{37}). His friends would say: 'No; you must not give way for a moment, or proper discipline becomes impossible.' On the other hand, no risk is run when the slave waits on his master, for that, as we say, 'is as it should be' (Luke $17^{7\text{ff.}}$); then the word 'parable' disappears. So the story of the shepherd with his lost sheep is a parable, while that of the woman with her lost coin is not; she ran no particular risk in cleaning her house. The widow who was brave enough to beard a powerful magistrate took a very serious risk, whereas the man who came borrowing loaves at midnight merely risked a refusal. I am not suggesting, of course, that Jesus Himself made such distinctions between one of His stories and another, only that there is a reason why Luke called some of the shorter stories in his collection 'parables', and some not. The work of God is most manifest in the lives of men and women when they are prepared to take risks for great ends, ignoring considerations of profit and loss. When, under certain pressures, or in face of some emergency, people act in this way, we are bidden by our Lord to look and look again, for here God is at work. As often—and how often it was so!—we saw or heard of men and women whom we should call unregenerate doing, daring, and enduring incredible things for each other in the blitz, we should have recognized that we were on holy ground, for we were watching God bringing good out of evil; the common bush was afire with God, and yet the bush was not consumed!

If this is so—and parable after parable tells the same story—it follows that our reforming energies are somewhat misdirected, when we base our anti-drink and anti-gambling campaigns on 'Safety first' or 'It's a mug's game'. I remember vividly the embarrassment of a Methodist group-leader who, when gambling was under discussion, asked the youngest member of the group which he was leading what she thought about bran-tubs at bazaars. He received the prompt reply: 'I should call them the first venture of faith'—I suppose there is an answer to this, but it is not so easy as might appear at first sight. Such arguments as 'It is dishonest to try to get something for nothing' or 'Gambling involves risking not merely your own happiness, but other people's', or 'It is mere selfishness to spend money, on your own pleasure, which should go to the support of your family or some good cause', by all means, but *not* 'It's dangerous'. When the substance of our exhortations amounts to 'always keep a hold of nurse for fear of catching something worse'—though we are not silly enough to put it like that—the most high-spirited of our young people will despise us, and—worse than that—we shall be going directly contrary to the spirit of our Lord's teaching.

The parable of the Rich Fool (Luke 12[16ff.]) expresses the same idea negatively. This hard-working farmer had, as Jesus said in another connexion, 'received his reward'; providence had crowned his praiseworthy industry with a bumper crop, and he had no more risks to run. When he had got it safely stowed away, we watch him playing for safety, the risk he is anxious to avoid consisting in any interference with the comfort of a well-earned retirement. Naturally he feels that his release from long hours and anxiety about the future constitutes an occasion for some kind of celebration. So he arranges for a banquet, and all possible precautions have been taken to make any interference with his plans unlikely, if not impossible. But just when he is ready to 'set in motion the mechanism of jollification'—as a colleague of mine once expressed it—the least expected of all gate-crashings takes place: God touches him on his shoulder, and says: 'They've come to ask for you tonight.' Who are meant by 'they' we are left to guess—most commentators content themselves with the cautious remark that this is an instance of the 'impersonal plural' (as in 'They're after you, my lad!'). This very sinister-sounding 'they' might refer, of course, to the undertakers or bearers who appear with such surprising and suspicious promptitude twice over in the story of Ananias and Sapphira. I have sometimes played with the idea that they are meant to stand for the rest of the human race whom he had ignored in his careful arrangements, as we say, 'You've got to join the great majority'! On further consideration, however, I am inclined to think that the fact—if indeed it was a fact—that he had committed the social and religious misdemeanour of eating his morsel alone,[2] would in that case have been more clearly stated, though it may be said to be implied. Perhaps the words which precede the parable ('Not in the surplus of his possessions does a man's true life consist'—Luke 12[15]) give us the clue. The soul only keeps itself alive by adventure of body, mind, or spirit, or all three; in other words, by its readiness at any moment to risk its security. A man can only really *possess* anything when he is sufficiently master of it at any moment to part with it for the sake of something better worth having, the possession of his own soul. As a friend of mine once put it in my hearing—he has now, strangely it may be thought, joined the Church of Rome—'When you come to a conclusion, you're dead.' Your 'come-outer' is ever your true pilgrim; like Jacob on his death-bed, he still has his staff in his hand, and is ready for another and yet more venturesome journey to round off the few and evil days of the years of 'his pilgrimage'.[3]

The story itself is based upon Ecclesiasticus 11[21], but what in the book of the older Jesus is a hasty sketch in the Gospel is a finished work of art, rounded, complete, and intensely dramatic;[4] everything ready, business affairs in perfect order, the well-spread table, the smooth service—and—nobody there!

Luke 12[21] ('So is every one who lays up treasure for himself, and is not rich toward God') is textually doubtful, and should probably be omitted.

As I mentioned on page 34, it is questionable—also for textual reasons—whether the sketch of the Pharisee and the publican at prayer (in Luke 18[9ff.]) should be counted in with Lucan parables.[5] It cannot be said to contain any suggestion of risk, though there is surprise in it. I propose to defer its consideration to a later chapter in which other Lucan stories told by Jesus are dealt with. The parable of the Unjust Judge and the Importunate Widow (Luke 18[1ff.]) presents us with a number of problems. Without the words which follow the story, words to which special attention is called by Jesus in 'Hear what the unjust judge says' (verse 6), it might well be little more than a doublet of the story

[2] Job 31[17].

[3] Hebrews 11[21].

[4] T. W. Manson (*The Sayings of Jesus*) mentions what he calls 'a perfect modern parallel' in Jung's *Analytical Psychology* (pp. 399ff.); and Toynbee's monumental *Study of History* might fairly be called an extension of the same theme.

[5] The words 'this parable' are omitted in the 'Western' text, and Dr. Hort taught us some time ago to take Western 'non-interpolations' seriously.

of the Importunate Friend (Luke $11^{5ff.}$). Our Lord's commentary may be paraphrased: 'Hear what the unjust judge says' (he has just confessed himself nagged and pestered into doing his duty for once).[6] 'And, as for God, can it be that He (like the judge) either will not, or cannot, avenge the wrongs of those who cry for reprisals to Him day and night? Is it that He is just putting up with the annoyance of their badgering, or that He is too forbearing with their enemies to fulfil His promises, or do the right thing by His clients? No, I tell you; He will avenge them speedily. Really, may not the true explanation be that the Son of Man *has* come ("and by His coming paved the way for the answer to *all* their prayers"), and does not seem likely to find genuine faith on the earth?'

The evangelist tells us that this parable was told 'that men should always pray and not grow weary', but our Lord's own comments imply that its real subject is the problem of seemingly unanswered prayer. The story then gives us a vivid picture of a situation only too familiar in the Middle East. A widow brings a case against one of those money-lenders who have always been one of the chief plagues of peasant life. The magistrate before whom the case comes is concerned solely for his own dignity and the perquisites of his office. But this time he is faced by a particularly persistent woman, who threatens to make herself an intolerable nuisance. The man against whom she is bringing the case has influential connexions, and is able to make it worth the presiding magistrate's while to quash the case, if he can. We must bear in mind the fact that the Romans (or Herod Antipas, if the case came up in Galilee) left civil law—that is, all cases in which the occupying power was not implicated and which did not involve a capital charge—in the hands of Jewish magistrates, when accused and accuser were both of Jewish nationality. Moreover, the law of Moses, as interpreted by the scribes, was particularly severe on the exaction of usurious interest by Jews at the expense of fellow-Jews, most of all when they were widows or orphans; so the law was on the woman's side, and both parties

[6] I feel sure that we must take the word translated 'longsuffering' (R.V.) in its natural sense. It might mean 'Is He really putting up with the nuisance their complaints cause Him?' But the strong word used here, which means rather 'magnanimous' or 'tolerant', suggests that what is meant is that God is exasperatingly easy with the persecutors of His chosen people. If this is so, we have a striking parallel with Jonah's complaint in Jonah $4^{1f.}$! Magnanimity, Jonah thought, is sometimes misapplied.

knew it. Three possibilities might have occurred to the cynic of the bench. One might have been the way of the dictator, the rough and ready method of 'elimination'. He was not a dictator, or anything of the sort, so that was out of the question. Another might have been an attempt at bribery, but that would have cost him money, and 'there is', he would say to himself, 'no limit to the demands of these people, if a man once gives way to them'. The third was to try to put her off with smooth words, promises that the matter would be inquired into in due course, though that would take time, and so on, in the hope that the woman would get tired of coming to court, or that something would happen to rid him of the nuisance. But he soon saw that this was getting him no farther; the only result of his assurances was that the widow became more and more violent, and he was in serious danger of 'losing face' over the business.[7] The one thing the Eastern official cannot afford is to 'lose face'. A Chinese missionary once told me that, when a certain type of Chinese woman has a grievance, she is not content with coming to court, but camps out on the magistrate's doorstep. Even if she is removed by the police, she can generally manage to make such a scene, and win so much popular support in doing so, as to succeed in making the official look ridiculous, and then more often than not, she gets her way. If he was not to be made a public laughing-stock, and lose his much-prized dignity for ever, the unjust judge in the parable had for once to do his obvious duty.

But it is by no means only in the Middle East that the business of getting one's own way by acquiring a 'nuisance value' has become a fine art; in British politics the Irish began it, and suffragettes carried the good work on. Then Hindus and Moslems

[7] The translation of Luke 18[5] in our versions ('lest by her continual coming she weary me') is tame, and does not harmonize with the only other example of the use of this colloquial word in the New Testament (1 Corinthians 9[27]). Surely Paul did not *tire himself out* to keep himself in order! The rendering 'weary me' seems to have been due to a natural desire to avoid the suggestion of a vulgarism on the lips of Jesus, but it is hardly credible that the magistrate actually feared assault and battery (the phrase should mean 'give [me] a black eye', as in 1 Corinthians 9[27] ['buffet']). 'Humiliate' or 'cause to lose face' seems to suit both passages, and the Greek word certainly has something to do with 'face'. I presume that the idea of weariness came from the observation that, when people are tired they tend to get dark shadows under their eyes. Field (*Notes on the New Testament*) accepts the translation 'weary' in Luke 18[5], but cannot give us any parallels from contemporary literature. I am inclined to think the rendering is the invention of ingenious but embarrassed commentators!

joined in the game, in order to drive the British Raj out of India, and now some of the Jews who have suffered more than any of the others, and have been patient immeasurably longer, have taken it up. It is tragic that they seem likely to have gained more by terrorism than they ever won by resignation.

The first suggestion made by the parable is: It is true that you can often get your own way by making yourself so objectionable to human authorities that in sheer desperation they give way; in actual fact, this often seems to be the *only* effective means of getting justice done. Irish Nationalists, the suffragettes, Indians and Jews have all used this method, and it has paid. Indeed, many of us who belong to none of these groups practise the method in a milder form. If we want anything from a Government Department, we fire a volley of postcards and telephone calls at the most accessible of its representatives, and, if the worst comes to the worst, get a question asked 'in the House'. This is in fact a generally accepted view of the facts of life—with human officials it seems to work when nothing else will. Be quiet and resigned, and nobody will take the slightest notice of you; make yourself thoroughly objectionable, and there is a chance of getting something done. But does this method work with God? Can we, to use a familiar phrase, 'storm the gates of Heaven with prayer'? But, before we go on to the discussion of this question, there is this to be said. It does not follow that the successes men obtain even in human affairs in this way give them much lasting satisfaction when they are achieved.

Are the Irish or the suffragettes really any happier for their triumphs? Are Indians and Jews likely to be? It may well be doubted. What the importunate widow was out for was vengeance, and undoubtedly she found some satisfaction in making the moneylender disgorge his ill-gotten gains. But we have heard a great deal about retribution in recent years, and the Nuremberg trials have given us our fill of it. Such gratification as the representatives of victims of the German concentration-camps have enjoyed has not lasted long, and it is not easy to see what permanent advantage anybody has got out of it all.

At this point Jesus turns aside from the general subject of 'unanswered prayer' and the question whether we can 'storm the gates of Heaven', to a particular example, the prayers for vengeance on their oppressors which have been offered for centuries by His own people, the Jews, God's elect. Persecution of Christians had not yet begun when He spoke, and 'cry to Him day and night' is in the present tense, not the future. Their sufferings had already been going on for centuries, and have continued spasmodically, it may be, but on a vaster scale and with immeasurably more ingenious and better-equipped cruelty ever since. When we consider the promises of redress and compensation made to them in such passages of Scripture as Isaiah 60—calmly appropriated since then by the Christian Church, as the chapter-headings in our Authorized Version show, but unquestionably first addressed to the remnant of Jewish people who had returned from exile in Babylon—and put beside them what has actually happened (their country occupied for centuries before and after Christ by Assyrians, Babylonians, Persians, Greeks, Romans, Turks, Arabs, British, indeed, by almost everybody except themselves), we see how tragic the problem of unanswered prayer must seem to the Zionists who, however mistaken we may think them to be, have had so very much to encourage their hopes in their and our Bible. They had, as they thought, fulfilled God's conditions, for they had, on their return from exile, utterly renounced the idolatry which had been the constant theme of prophetic denunciations, and the disloyalties of past generations had surely been atoned for by this time; they had 'received double for all their sins'. For centuries now their cry had been going up to God, and what had been the result of it all? They had been assured that they were to be the envy of all nations (Isaiah $60^{14f.}$); centuries after the promise had been given, they were still the most despised and hated people in the world! It must have seemed that they were faced with an alternative terrible to contemplate: either God would not, or He could not, fulfil His promises! Was He, after all, like some harassed Prime Minister, struggling vainly against insurmountable difficulties? Was He merely putting up with the nuisance of prayers He could not answer, too kind-hearted, as Jonah had said, to deal once and for all with the heathen nations who were trampling them in the dust? Or was it that He had forsaken His people, and if so, why? Jesus answers all such bitter surmisings with a blank negative. God is not only ready to avenge them; He has done so already many times, and will soon do so again, but only on condition that they are prepared to accept their calling to be a servant-nation;[8] that is the way, and the only way, to happiness, liberty, or power.[9] God will destroy their oppressors, as He always had done—Assyria, Babylon had disappeared, and the rest would follow—but the discomfiture of their enemies will bring them no nearer to the end of their troubles, unless they are doing the work they were sent into the world to do. The promises, like the threatenings of God, are, and must always in the nature of the case, be conditional.

The clue to the acknowledged mystery of unanswered prayer, Jesus finally declares, is the lack of adequate response to the answer *God has already given.* The 'bolt from the blue', which we have learned to expect, comes, as usual, in the last sentence of all. Whereas in our relations with men our difficulty in getting wrongs righted is due to the 'law's delays', and the only way open to the oppressed seems to be the acquisition of some kind of 'nuisance value', in our relations with God *His* difficulty is due to *our* lack of vision; the Jews and all the rest of us cannot see that He has *already* answered all our prayers in the gift of 'the Son of Man'. To put the matter in colloquial speech: in our dealings with men we have to do the prodding; in God's dealings with us He has to do the prodding.

Whether the phrase 'the Son of Man' means Jesus Himself, or, as others think,[10] it has a collective sense (see Daniel $7^{13ff.}$), and, as used by Jesus, stands for Christ and His Church, makes no essential difference to the meaning of the sentence: 'Only,[11] may the fact not be that the Son of Man *has* come, and is not going to find true faith' (of the indomitable kind represented by the importunate widow) 'on the earth?' The story of the Unjust Judge and the Importunate Widow *is* a parable, because it introduces us to a new and amazing truth, amazing because it transforms and transfigures our whole human situation, as the 'Verilies' and 'Verily, verilies' do, but the companion-story of the Importunate Neighbour (Luke $11^{5ff.}$) does not, re-emphasizing, as it does,

[8] A 'servant-nation' movement is already in being, and in this Jews and Christians are joining hands to find a way of fulfilling the age-long vocation of Israel. Perhaps for the present there is little that they can do except help to keep the idea alive, but it is a fine gesture.

[9] Mark $10^{35ff.}$

[10] As I am inclined to think, following suggestions made in private conversation by Mr. J. R. Coates, and afterwards reinforced by reading T. W. Manson's *Teaching of Jesus*.

[11] The word here translated 'only' several times introduces the *final and decisive* pronouncement of Jesus on the subject under discussion (see e.g. Luke 6^{35}, 11^{41}, 13^{33}).

a truth already familiar, however valuable its repetition may be, for it is expressed already in such a proverb as 'If you don't at first succeed, try, try again'. This new truth is that God has already answered all our prayers, did we but know it, and that we are hammering at an open door. If the answer already given has not produced the effect we desire upon the situation in which we find ourselves, that is because even religious men have not realized that God has already given, and is giving, all that He has to give in the Incarnation. Now He can only wait for our eyes to be opened. 'Show us the Father, Lord', says Philip, and Jesus answers, 'He that hath seen Me hath seen the Father' (John 14^{9}). We pray for the coming of the Kingdom, and the Kingdom has come; for the gift of the Holy Spirit, and the Holy Spirit is ours for ever; some of us clamour for a Second Coming, and the First has already answered our prayers by anticipation! The only question awaiting an answer is: What is the Church and the world making of the unspeakable gifts which are already in their possession?

The last of the stories peculiar to Luke which he calls 'parables' ($19^{11ff.}$) presents the expositor with a different kind of problem. Here, by some twist in the tradition, two separate stories have become entangled together. One concerns a nobleman who went to a 'far country' to get for himself a kingdom, and return (verse 12). This 'plot' seems to be continued in verses 14–27, though it has become almost inextricably confused with the other which deals with a master who had ten slaves, and entrusted them with the use of a sum of money while he was away, giving to each of them one pound.[12] The first is based upon the fact that Archelaus[13] went to Rome in 4 B.C. to push his claim under Herod the Great's will to succeed to the title of 'king'. He was intensely unpopular with the Jews, and an insurrection in favour of Antipas, his brother, led to the sending of a deputation led by Antipas himself to the capital to oppose Archelaus' claim. When Archelaus won his case (though he was never more than 'ethnarch'), he returned and slaughtered as many of his antagonists as he could lay hands on. It is incredible that Jesus should have quoted an incident in the career of this most bloodthirsty of all the Herods as any kind of analogy to His own mission, and I am

[12] The same kind of confusion can be seen in Matthew $22^{1ff.}$ (see p. 54 *infra*).
[13] Josephus, *Antiquities of the Jews*, XVII (Niese's Edition).

inclined to suggest that Luke $19^{12, 14f., 27}$ are all that is left of a *contrast* between the Son of Herod and the Son of Man. This might well be the case, if we could link the original parable with verse 10 ('The Son of Man is come to seek and save that which was lost') which is appended to the preceding paragraph (the story of Zaccheus). Then the original parable might be thought to have run something like this: '*Unlike* Archelaus who went to a far country to obtain the right to destroy his enemies, Jesus has come to a far country to seek and save the prodigal.'[14] We should then have at once the needed counterpart of the story of the Prodigal Son, and an illustration in 'parable' of the saying: 'The Son of Man came not to destroy men's lives, but to save them' (Luke 9^{56}). But I confess that there is a good deal of guess-work in this reconstruction; it is the best I can make of a passage which has puzzled me more than any other in the Synoptic Gospels.

The plot of the other parable is quite straightforward. It reminds us closely of the parable of the Talents (Matthew $25^{14ff.}$), though the details are so different in the two Gospels that it is not easy to believe that they came from the same source ('Q').[15] In Luke there are *ten* slaves, though we only hear of what three of them did with their money, whereas in the First Gospel there are only *three* all through. In Luke all the slaves start with *equal* chances, but the two successful slaves end with unequal rewards; in the First Gospel they start with *unequal* opportunities (five, two, talents) and end with *equal* commendation. The protest against 'carrying coals to Newcastle' in verse 25 is also peculiar to Luke, but perhaps is not part of the original text. One's first impression is that the First Evangelist has tidied up and greatly improved an unusually mechanical original (found in Luke), but the Matthew-parable seems so much more nearly akin to what I have learned to think is the spirit of Jesus, that I hesitate to accept this view. On the whole I prefer to leave the study of this theme till we come to the version in the First Gospel, only noticing here that the true parabolic 'bolt from the blue' is found in both Gospels (Luke 19^{26}=Matthew 25^{29}), and that the other element (the 'risk' motif) is also paramount in both.

Dr. C. H. Dodd maintains that all parables properly so called

[14] Who had already taken 'his journey' there (Luke $15^{11ff.}$).

[15] Of course, the same phenomenon occurs elsewhere, e.g. in Luke $14^{16ff.}$; Matthew $22^{1ff.}$, and to some extent—though not so noticeably—in Luke $15^{1ff.}$; Matthew 18^{12}.

are taken from actual life, and that even the story of the Wicked Husbandmen, called a 'parable' in all three Synoptics, falls into this category. The incident it depicts, he says, is quite realistic, for when large estates were held by foreigners, refusal of the rent might well be a prelude to murder. On the other hand, I find it hard to resist the impression that the story has been made to fit a particular event, the rejection and murder of Jesus by the chief priests, and the consequent transference of the Kingdom to the Gentiles. It does not seem likely that any landlord in his senses would risk his son's life, when he was aware that some of his emissaries had already been done to death.[16] At any rate, this 'parable' stands in a class by itself; none of the others (except possibly the parable of the Fig-tree spared a year longer—Luke 13$^{6f.}$) fits a definite historical situation with such neatness.[17] For this reason among others I am inclined to think that this 'parable' did not come from the lips of Jesus, though it is taken from Mark into the First and Third Gospels. But it certainly contains one characteristic of a true parable-surprise.

[16] Mark 12^{5}. Luke (20$^{9ff.}$) sees the unlikelihood of this, and suggests that the husbandmen had not actually committed murder before the arrival of the heir.

[17] Matthew (21^{39}) and Luke (20^{15}) intensify the tidiness of the allegory by changing Mark's 'slew him and cast him out of the vineyard' to 'cast him out of the vineyard and slew him'; Jesus was crucified outside the city walls.

CHAPTER FIVE

PARABLES ABOUT PEOPLE IN THE FIRST GOSPEL

In the First Gospel, after Chapter 13, parables are generally introduced by the formula, 'Therefore the Kingdom of Heaven is like'; as this formula occurs five times in Chapter 13, in which the similes introduced in this way are expressly called 'parables', we may take it that all narratives about men and women introduced with this formula are also thought of as parables. In $7^{24ff.}$ (the so-called parable of the two householders) the introductory formula is, 'Therefore everyone who hears these words . . . shall be like', and in 13^{52}, 'Every scribe who is also a disciple . . . is like'. Perhaps, then, we should deal with these two cases under a separate heading. Matthew $21^{28ff.}$, though not introduced by the usual formula, but by the words 'What do you think?', should be counted in with Matthaean parables, because in verse 33 we have the words 'another parable', implying that there has been one already. The story of the Reckless Slave bears no suggestion that it is a parable at all in the strict sense of the word, and is only dealt with in this chapter because of its obvious relation to the parable of the cautious slave (the talents), which is.

In Matthew $25^{1ff.}$ the usual formula is altered to, 'Then the Kingdom of Heaven *shall* be like'; though the parable—or allegory (?)—of the Ten Bridesmaids has many of the marks of a true parable, the fact that it has an eschatological setting may be regarded as removing it from our list of stories of actual life.[1] As will be evident when we come to this parable, I am not sure if this same thing is true of Dives and Lazarus in Luke's Gospel: both stories begin with a scene taken from actual life in this world, but the 'parable' of the Bridesmaids takes it as an illustration of a future consummation, and in the allegory of the Rich Man and Lazarus the first act of the drama is enacted in this world, the second in another.

[1] It is true that other parables are given an eschatological application (of 'The darnel in the wheat' and 'the drag-net'), but in these cases the eschatology only appears in the explanation of the parables, not in the parable itself.

In this chapter, then, we are to discuss the twin parables of the Hidden Treasure (which we might call 'ungotten minerals') and the Pearl of Great Price (Matthew $13^{44ff.}$), the Unmerciful Slave ($18^{23ff.}$), the Labourers in the Vineyards ($20^{1ff.}$), the Two Sons ($21^{28ff.}$), the Man without the Wedding-garment ($22^{1ff.}$), and the Talents ($25^{11ff.}$).

In the parable of the Hidden Treasure we are not told whether the man who found it was looking for buried treasure, or came across it by accident. If we will, we may imagine that he was a peasant ploughing on a plot of land which he rented from a landlord, when his ploughshare grates against something hard which is not a stone. As he stoops down to look he catches sight of the glint of gold. Maybe he has heard tales of treasure buried in the neighbourhood; such rumours are common in the Middle East, and seeking for it is a favourite occupation of the *fellaheen.*[2] Hurriedly he marks the spot with a twig, and kicks back the earth over the place. When his day's work is finished he hastens home, and counts his savings eagerly; 'Yes', he thinks to himself, 'I may have just enough.' The steward on whom he waits next morning is surprised, perhaps, and inclined to be suspicious—what does this fellow want with just this bit of land? But he decides to sell, as it is poor, thin soil anyhow, and of no special value to the master, and determines to make the fellow pay heavily. After a good deal of haggling a bargain is struck and the labourer, hardly able yet to believe in his good fortune, hurries back to the field, digs up the gold, and smuggles it home.

Turning from imagery to meaning, the surprise which is the heart of all our Lord's parables is to be found in the fact that there are such ungotten minerals available in this world for poor labouring men. They are hidden, it is true, but only just below the surface, and at any moment they may come upon them. We all know that we can have treasure in Heaven, but this is treasure hidden in the field of workaday life where poor men and women have to toil and sweat for bare subsistence. The treasure is the 'Kingdom of Heaven', 'infinite riches in a little room'. I know

[2] I was assured by one of my students who served in German East Africa in the 1914–18 war that he had watched them doing so, lifting up stones in the field and groping in decayed tree-stumps round its edge (sometimes indeed cutting into them to make a larger hole) in their frantic search. He thought that this custom might well be the explanation of the Oxyrhynchus Saying of the Lord: 'Raise the stone, and you shall find Me; cleave the wood, and there am I'; as we might say: 'leave no corner unexplored, no stone unturned.'

it is commonly held that the 'Kingdom of Heaven' is only a characteristically reverent Jewish way of saying the 'Kingdom of God', but, as I have read and reread the First Gospel in recent years, I have been coming to wonder whether the two expressions —the 'Kingdom of Heaven' (which, of course, is confined to the First Gospel) and the 'Kingdom of God'—are regarded by the evangelist as exactly synonymous. For the fact is that he does not *always* turn the 'Kingdom of God', which no doubt he found in 'Q', into his favourite 'Kingdom of Heaven'. In 12^{28} and 21^{31} he allows 'Kingdom of God' to stand. This might be an accident, but it is surely significant that in these two passages he is concerned with the Kingdom as a fact which is independent of human recognition of it, whereas elsewhere there is a complex of ideas, not only the fact, but the consequences of men's recognition of and acceptance of the fact being involved in his use of the phrase.

However that may be, in this parable both ideas—recognition of a fact and acceptance of its implications—are combined; the peasant sees the treasure and sells all that he has to make the treasure his own.

My father, Dr. G. G. Findlay, was, I believe, the first expositor to point out that the parable of the Great Price is not a mere doublet of that of the Hidden Treasure; no one except his son and his students has, so far as I am aware, taken much notice of the observation, but it is none the less true for all that. Whereas in the parable of the Hidden Treasure the 'Kingdom' is the object found, in the Pearl of Great Price it is the Finder. Dr. T. W. Manson may be thinking of a perversion of this theory when he remarks: 'It is one of the curiosities of New Testament interpretation that the pearl in the parable came to be identified, not with the Kingdom, but with Christ Himself.'[3] But surely this is natural. It may be true, as Otto wrote in a memorable sentence, that 'Jesus did not preach Himself as bringing the Kingdom, but the Kingdom as bringing Him with it', but how did the recognition of the fact that God was at work in the world and in their own lives dawn upon the followers of Jesus, except through His coming? Whatever distinction *He* made between Himself and the Kingdom, *they* would for all practical purposes

[3] *The Sayings of Jesus*, p. 197. In G. G. Findlay's exposition, the Kingdom is not the pearl, but the pearl-merchant.

identify the Lord and the Kingdom He proclaimed, and surely they were right! In the parable of the Pearl of Great Price, at least, 'it' (the Kingdom) has become 'He'. We should not, in seeking Him, be called upon to give and hazard all we have, if He, to seek and save us, had not already surrendered all that He possessed—and how much more He had to give than we! The saying, 'He that seeks to save His soul shall lose it' is set in the context of the journey to the Cross, and applied to the Lord Himself as well as to His followers.[4] For of Him it is true, as of the rest of us, that, 'Except a corn of wheat fall into the ground and die, it abides alone: but, if it die, it bears much fruit.'[5] The treasure is in our field, but who lived and died to put it there? The mystery about the Kingdom is at last disclosed, so far as it can be set forth in speech; this is the crowning surprise—a 'bolt from the blue' indeed.

The fact that the other element in the parable-idea—that of risk—is present in these twin-parables needs little comment. Indeed, no lasting friendship is possible even between men if one of the friends holds anything back, and this is true of both parties even when God and man come together; each must give himself away 'for better for worse, for richer, for poorer'. It is not enough that God should visit us, and then that the opening heavens should close again; He must come to stay. So, in the First Gospel, 'God with us' passes into 'I with you—*all the days*' (1^{23}, 28^{20}). Mutual surrender follows mutual discovery; but the difference between God and man is as great as ever, for we could never find Him unless He had already found us, and He could never have found us, if He had not 'emptied Himself' before He came. When Paul wrote, 'He was *found* in fashion as a man', perhaps we ought to lay the emphasis on the word 'found'; men were able to discover that He was divine because He was so human.[6] This idea runs through the New Testament, but it is specially prominent in the First Gospel, as can easily be seen, if we note the passages in which the word 'find' occurs. Finding Jesus we find 'the path which leads to life', we find ourselves, we

[4] Some ancient MSS. read (in Mark 8^{36}): 'What shall it profit *the* Man if He gain the whole world and lose his own soul?' This might mean 'mankind' (as in Matthew $12^{43, 45}$) or 'the Heavenly Man'. If the latter, the saying might well mean: 'Is it worth while to gain the world, if I must lose My life to do so?'

[5] John 12^{24}.

[6] Compare Luther's great saying: 'Take hold of Christ as a man, and you will discover that He is God.'

find hidden treasure, we find 'rest for souls', and so on. To put it in a sentence—the finder of the hidden treasure sold all that he had after he had found it; the finder of the pearl sold all that He had before He had found it.[7]

I doubt whether the story of the Unmerciful Slave (Matthew $18^{21ff.}$) should be counted as one of the parables. The elements of risk and surprise, though present, are not central to its theme, and the story is obviously devised to fit a particular situation. It is possible—though not perhaps very likely—that a king would forgive a slave a debt of roughly two million pounds. T. W. Manson[8] suggests that the numerical signs for ten and a thousand have been confused, and that the debt amounted to ten talents (about £2,000). This is possible, for such confusions are not uncommon in contemporary literature. But may not the word translated 'ten thousand' simply stand for 'any number of' as in 1 Corinthians 4^{15} ('though you have *any number of* Christian schoolmasters, you have not got many fathers')? It is true that favourite slaves of Oriental monarchs were put in charge of vast estates, and that some of the richest men under the empire were or had been slaves. Nor can there be any doubt about the effectiveness of the story for its purpose; I know from experience that there are few passages from Scripture—apart from the Sermon on the Mount and the Epistle of James—that carry their meaning so unmistakably to the average congregation. The phrase, 'So also shall My heavenly Father do unto you' (i.e. 'hand you over to the tormentors'), should be taken in the same sense as: 'Verily I say to you, you shall not come out [of prison] until you have paid the last farthing'[9]—'the torturers' standing for that hell on earth into which a man is plunged when he is left with his grievances for sole company. Such a straightforward statement needs little comment, and the story carries its own message unanswerably home.

The next example on our list (Matthew $20^{1ff.}$), though, like the last, it fits the situation with nice precision, may properly be called a 'parable', for it contains what deserves to be called a 'bolt from the blue'. In my book, *Jesus in the First Gospel* (long out of print) I called it 'Last come, first served', and can find no

[7] This is clear enough in the original Greek—in Matthew 13, verse 44, we have 'He sells', in verse 45, 'He has sold'.
[8] *The Sayings of Jesus*, p. 213.
[9] Matthew 5^{26}, Luke 12^{59}.

better title now. As is usual in the First Gospel, it fits its context like a glove. Peter has just asked what reward those who had left home to follow Jesus, as the 'rich young ruler' had declined to do, were to have, and has been assured that they would get back at compound interest all that they had forsaken for His Name's sake (19[29]).[10] The parable with which we are concerned seems to be appended to this promise as a kind of caveat, to check undue exuberance. Before the desirable consummation just described in such glowing terms arrives, there are to be many ups and downs, many unexpected reversals, for the only way to be first is to be willing at any time to become last. It is difficult not to associate this parable in our minds with the story of the two sons of Zebedee asking—either in their own persons (Mark 10[35]) or through their mother Salome (Matthew 20[20])—for the first two places in the 'glory' (Mark) or the 'Kingdom' (Matthew) of Jesus, especially if we are allowed (with the Old Latins and the Old Syriac version) in Mark 10[40] to read 'for others it has been prepared by My Father' instead of 'it is for those for whom it has been prepared by My Father'. Not Peter, James, and John, but two crucified outcasts were nearest to Jesus on the Cross which was His glory. I think T. W. Manson is right in his suggestion[11] that the real point of the parable is that in the Kingdom questions of precedence have ceased to matter, because the love of God cannot be doled out in appropriate doses according to merit. 'There is such a thing as the twelfth part of a *denarius*—it is called a "pandion"; there is no such thing as a twelfth part of the love of God.' At the same time, it is also true that the first group of workmen bargained with their employer for a *denarius* for the day—then the normal man's wage for a day's work on the land—while those who came in at the last hour left the question of their reward to him. That this is a true story I see no reason to doubt.[12]

[10] Neither the First Evangelist nor Luke says, as Mark (10[30]) does, that they will be rewarded *in the same coinage*, with 'persecutions', which seem to be included among the rewards of service as a kind of extra bonus. Variations between the Synoptics are specially interesting here: Mark has, 'For Me and the gospel' (or, as some scholars think, 'For the gospel's sake'); Luke, 'For the sake of the Kingdom of God'; Matthew, 'For My name's sake.'

[11] *The Sayings of Jesus*, p. 220.

[12] A Rabbinic parable provides us with a piquant contrast in application. Its plot is the same, in as far as a man who worked only one hour is paid as much as those who had worked all day. In the Rabbinic parable, however, the reply to the aggrieved workman is to the effect that he had done more work in one hour than the others

The short parable in Matthew 21[28ff.], like that of the labourers in the vineyard, involves a complete reversal of accepted values; indeed, so much is this so, that a succession of bewildered copyists have found themselves unable to believe that Jesus could have said what the text before them declared that He said. To Western minds the meaning of the parable, whatever we make of the comment which follows it (21[31f.]), is straightforward enough. The Pharisees made professions of obedience to God's will but, when it came to following the lead of Jesus, turned sulky and would not fall into line; the publicans, on the other hand, who made no professions of piety, did follow Jesus: the people who said they would go into the vineyard did not go, and the people whose whole manner of life said 'No' to the call of God, did. But a series of various readings going back to the earliest MSS. and versions of the Gospel we possess proves that early copyists, themselves Orientals, did not find this conclusion by any means obvious.

Some MSS. say 'the first' in verse 31, others 'the last', while many reverse the order of the sons, in order to agree with the comment made in verse 32. It is probable that the difficulty created by verse 32 was partly, at least, responsible for the textual chaos which is the result of each copyist in turn trying to clear up the confusion left by the last, and only adding to it by his efforts. For verse 32 reads: 'John came to you following the God-appointed course (this is the meaning of "righteousness" in the First Gospel —see 3[15]), and you did not believe him, but the publicans and harlots did believe him; but you (when you saw this happen) were not induced by remorse to believe him.' It is certainly very confusing; our natural inference would have been, as we have seen, to say that the elder son stands for the Pharisee who was polite but disobedient, the younger for the publican who refused churlishly, but actually obeyed—but this scheme is made impossible by verse 32, where the Pharisees are charged with behaving like the younger son, not the elder, because they say 'No', but, unlike the younger son, do not change their minds and go after all! It is likely that the copyist saw this difficulty, and tried unavailingly to make things fit. But it seems likely, too, that the answers made by the listeners to the original discussion were not unanimous. We

had done all day! The parable, we are informed, was suggestive of the premature death of a promising young Rabbi who had done as much in his short life as his older contemporaries had done in a long one.

must bear in mind the fact that such public discussions, taking the form of question and answer, with a crowd of spectators joining in and shouting their own answers,[13] were a feature of life in the towns of the Middle East in those days. That there might well be an honest difference of opinion about the behaviour of the two sons is shown by the story told by a missionary. He told this parable to a crowd of Palestinians only a few years ago exactly as it appears in the First Gospel—and then put the question: 'Who did the will of his father?' To his great surprise the crowd unanimously answered: 'The man who said he would go, and did not.' When they were asked why, they said: 'A day's work in the vineyard is a little thing, but to say "No" to your father's beard is a grievous sin.' Popular opinion in Syria evidently thinks good manners more important than practical obedience.[14] What has become almost a commonplace with us was clearly a shock to those who first heard it. Verse 32 is either a comment added editorially by the evangelist (like Luke's 'He spake a parable (to teach us) that men should pray and not faint') or—more probably—a retort by Jesus Himself to a defiant answer shouted back by the Pharisees ('You were neither polite like the elder son, nor obedient like the younger').

With our next parable difficulties are of a different kind. It is evident that the same sort of thing has happened in Matthew $22^{1ff.}$ as in Luke $19^{11ff.}$ (the parable of the Pounds): two distinct parables have become entangled with one another in the tradition. In this case one is parallel with the story told by Jesus at a Pharisee's house in Luke $14^{16ff.}$, only here we are concerned with a prince's wedding, in Luke with a private dinner. The other would seem to be a variant of the allegory of the wicked husbandmen which preceded it in the First Gospel. Only fragments of this parable are left in verses 6 and 7 (Matthew 22), which fit in very awkwardly with what has gone before. They read: 'And the rest laid hold of his slaves, outraged them and slew them. And the king was angry, and sending his armies, destroyed those murderers, and burnt their city', describing what seems a most

[13] In default of such entertainments as football and cricket and racing, the Jewish public found a certain satisfaction for its sporting instincts in public debate. Much of the argument at cross-purposes which makes difficult reading of long passages in the Fourth Gospel, reflects the atmosphere of such discussions.

[14] In Ecclesiasticus 19^{21} two MSS. read: 'A slave that says to his lord, "I will not do according to thy will", even though he afterwards (changes his mind and) does so, angers him who keeps him.'

unlikely proceeding and so marring the realism of the story, for why should you kill slaves whose only offence is that they have asked you out to dinner? They fit the destruction of Jerusalem by the Roman army, but do *not* fit the story to which they are attached. Denney thought that they were added by a Christian preacher; Charles that they were added by the evangelist himself after the fall of Jerusalem. Possibly, as I have suggested, they come from another parable with a 'Wisdom' colouring (compare Proverbs 9[2ff.]: 'She (Wisdom) hath killed her beasts; she hath mingled her wine . . . she hath sent forth her maidens; she cries in the public places of the city, "Whoso is simple, let him come in hither" ') which has affected the description of the king's invitation and colours its language. In the original parable, Wisdom's messengers were set at nought and shamefully treated, with the consequences described in verse 7. That such a parable was quite possible we may judge from Luke 11[49]: 'Therefore the *Wisdom of God* said, I am sending prophets and apostles, and some of them they shall kill and persecute.' If we detach the two narratives (Wisdom's call and the Prince's wedding) we get a coherent and effective narrative. The Herods were unpopular at this time—and royal functions were often boycotted by the Pharisees.

A word is still extant in Arabic which means a garment offered by one's king or sheikh—to refuse such a garment offered by one's liege lord is regarded as *lèse-majesté*, and to accept one from the monarch of another country, or sheikh of another tribe, is tantamount to high treason to your own. This latter fact is probably the true explanation of the unpleasant story about Elisha and Gehazi in 2 Kings 5[25-27]. Gehazi's chief sin in Elisha's estimation was not that he told a lie, but that he accepted 'two changes of garments' from Naaman, the representative of the King of Syria. We notice how careful Elisha himself is to be under no obligation to Naaman (verse 16). 'Is it a time', says Elisha, 'to receive money and *garments*?' (the 'olive-yards and vineyards', etc., which follow constitute a mere oratorical flourish, for Gehazi had actually received none of these things). Elisha does not call Gehazi a liar—though he was one—but a traitor. When we realize that 'treason' is still known as 'leprosy' by the Arabs—who preserve many more Semitic customs and ideas than does the modern Jew who has become cosmopolitan—we may legitimately suspect that 'he went out of his presence a leper as white as snow' simply means 'a double-dyed traitor', and get rid once and for all the horrible suggestion that Gehazi and his children were smitten with leprosy because Gehazi told a lie. In spite of the fact, however, that the story of the man who refused to wear a wedding-garment may be taken from actual life, I suspect that it ought not to be called a 'parable' in the proper sense of the word. It seems to be so exactly fitted to the case of one individual—Judas Iscariot—that it perhaps deserves the name of 'allegory' rather than 'parable'. That it is not unknown for a man to be thrown bodily out into the street from a dining-room window is proved by the experience of a friend of mine who, on going up to the window of a house in old Jerusalem in which a feast was taking place, was forced to draw back hastily by the fact that a body came hurtling through the window. The man fell into the street, says my friend, picked himself up with a curse and took himself off down a dark side-street cursing and gnashing his teeth.[15] It is really the word 'comrade' which appears in verse 12 (Matthew 22) that makes me wonder whether this part of the 'parable' is not addressed to Judas. The same word—which seems to mean 'table-companion'—*is* addressed to Judas *Iscariot*[16] in Matthew 26^{50}.

It is common knowledge by this time, it may be hoped, that drinking-vessels have been discovered in various places in the Middle East all with this motto round the foot of the cup: 'Comrade, why are you here? Rejoice!' It follows that when Jesus said to Judas, 'Comrade, why are you here?' (A.V.; the R.V. has, quite unnecessarily, 'Comrade, do that for which thou art come!'), He was almost certainly quoting the motto on the Holy Grail itself, from which Judas had been drinking in His company only an hour or two before. Working back from Matthew 26^{50} to 22^{12}, and bearing in mind the fact that the only occurrences of the word 'comrade'[17] are Matthew 20^{13}, 22^{12}, 26^{50},

[15] Binding 'by the hands and the feet' was scarcely necessary, and we should perhaps accept the old Syriac and Western reading: 'Take him up by the hands and feet.'

[16] Or perhaps we should read 'Scarioth', as in Western MSS., which reminds us of the word '*sicarii*' (Aramaic: '*Scarioth*') which appears in Acts 21^{38}, and is translated 'assassins', but is used by Josephus in the milder sense of 'temple-zealots', a Judaean sect fanatically devoted to the Temple. The real reason for the betrayal may have been the fact that Jesus prophesied the destruction of the Temple (Mark 13^{2}).

[17] With the doubtful exception of a various reading in Matthew 11^{16} ('comrades' for 'others'—*hetairois* for *heterois*). The translation 'Friend' is misleading, because that represents another Greek word used, for instance, in Luke 14^{10}.

we surmise that Jesus habitually called Judas 'Comrade'.[18] Judas is in danger of being dismissed as Gehazi was by Elisha, and on the same ground—treason; with 'Cast him into the *outer darkness*' we may compare 'Jesus said (to Judas), What thou doest, do quickly, and Judas went out, and it was night' (John 13[30]). But it follows that, if we are right in thinking that this part of the story was expressly directed to Judas, it can hardly be called a 'parable', and should be put in the same category as, for instance, the fig-tree spared a year longer. Jesus is not here describing something which He had Himself observed, a scene taken from actual life which revealed what God was doing in and with men and women, but adapting a story of something which may or may not have happened to the case of a particular individual; in spite of 22[12], this episode of the man without a wedding-garment is *not* a parable of the Kingdom. A parable of the Kingdom is told for the truth it reveals, not for the truth which can be read into it.

Of course, all this does not necessarily mean that the story as it stands cannot have come from Jesus; far from it, for it is hardly conceivable that Jesus should have left Judas without warning of the danger He was in.

Leaving out of account the episode of the man who was thrown out of the banqueting-chamber on the one hand, and verses 6 and 7 on the other, we are left with a straightforward parable closely related to Luke 14[16ff.], the chief difference being that, in Luke, the slaves are sent out first into the streets and alleys of the city and then into the highways and byways of the countryside, whereas in the First Gospel they are sent to the 'partings of the main-roads', by which are meant the broad spaces outside the city gates where the roads meet before the city is entered; a kind of bottle-neck where, as all travellers in the Middle East know, a swarm of beggars congregates to beg for baksheesh from all those who come up to the gate. There they were certain to find plenty of people who would be only too glad of a free meal.

[18] Perhaps because he had been His first companion, the Gehazi to His Elisha. In Mark 14[10] the reading '*the* one of the twelve', referring to Judas, is accepted by Nestle and von Soden; it should mean 'the first of the twelve'. Judas has been sent down to the bottom of the class for misbehaviour! What an example of 'The first shall be last'! This accounts for the constant discussions about precedence among the twelve. The leader ('*one* of them' in Matthew 20[13]) of the aggrieved workmen whom the master addresses as 'Comrade' may also have represented Judas, who had been in the field long before Peter, James, and John, the favoured three.

Luke emphasizes social and physical distinctions ('the poor, the maimed, the halt, the blind'), the First evangelist moral distinctions ('both bad and good'). This is a note characteristic of the First Gospel (see also 13[47]: 'fish *of every kind*'). The First evangelist always shows himself well aware that 'Christianity is *the* religion for all poor devils'.

The parable of the talents (Matthew 25[14ff.]) is not actually called a 'parable' by the First evangelist, though it may be regarded as sharing the introduction to the chapter ('Then shall the Kingdom of Heaven be likened to', etc.) in verse 1. But it is really a companion to the story of the Reckless Slave which ends Chapter 24, and it will be convenient to deal with them together, though one is a 'parable' in the sense in which we have defined the word, and the other is not. Both are concerned with the Second Coming, one describing a slave who ignored the fact that his master was coming back to call him to account, while the other could not think of anything else. Indeed, it might be said that all four 'parables', if for convenience we call them all by that name, are connected together, the parable of the Bridesmaids and the Sheep and the Goats describing two different ways in which we can be prepared for the great emergency when it comes; the Reckless Slave and the Talents two ways in which it is possible to be completely unprepared for it. Both the Bridesmaids and the Sheep and Goats are coming up for consideration in a later chapter, so for the moment we will concentrate on the other two.

The portrait of the reckless slave (Matthew 24[48ff.], Luke 12[45ff.]) cannot be called a 'parable', but may well be a sketch from life all the same. It is clearly founded on the story of Ahikar, to which I have already referred in Chapter Three. In the Arabic version of that famous household-tale we read (IV.15), 'And Naidan began to seize the maid-servants and slaves of his uncle Haiqâr (Ahikar), and bound and tortured them and drubbed them with a sore drubbing', and in VIII.38 (when Haiqâr restored to his office has administered a long and cutting rebuke to Naidan) we read, 'And when Naidan heard that speech from his uncle Haiqâr, he swelled up immediately . . . and he was torn, and his belly burst asunder . . . and he perished, and died' (compare 'He shall *cut him asunder*' in Matthew 24[51], Luke 12[46], which is evidently not to be taken literally). In the Greek version Ahikar becomes Aesop, of *Aesop's Fables*! He appears again in the Book of Tobit ($1^{21f.}$, 2^{10}, 11^{18}), and there are obvious reminiscences of the story of Ahikar in the Book of Daniel.[19]

The sin of the reckless slave was that he regarded the office to which, like Naidan, he had been appointed by favour as his own property, ignoring the fact that he must render account for his trusteeship to his master. Any Church dignitary or popular preacher who comes to think of the Church as the sphere in which he can display his own administrative powers or gifts and graces for the advancement of his career is his modern representative, for there are other ways of 'bullying the menservants and maid-servants' than drubbing them 'with a sore drubbing': we can overawe them with the brilliance of our gifts.

The cautious slave (in the parable of the Talents) went to the other extreme, and he too has his counterparts in the modern Church: they can think and talk of nothing but the Second Coming, and do little else but wait and count the days. Like them, he could make a better case for himself than the reckless slave; after all, it was not his own money to play with, and even bankers in those days were not always to be trusted. Speculation is a dangerous business, most of all when one is risking trust-money. Surely 'safety first' was the right policy, when other people's money was at stake. The words he uses of his master are 'hard' in the First Gospel, 'austere' in Luke. The word translated 'hard' means what we colloquially call 'a nigger-driver'. Luke's word ('austere') does not occur again in the New Testament, and is perhaps resorted to because Luke was doubtful about the propriety of the application of the harsher word to Jesus.

We must, however, beware of suggesting that the master in this case '*represents*' Jesus; by so doing we turn a parable into an allegory, and land ourselves into a hundred and one needless expository difficulties. The point is rather that in everyday human life, the kind of transaction which took place between master and slave, for instance, we can if we will see some deep and abiding truth concerning the relations of God and man. The Good Samaritan does not *represent* Jesus, any more than the father of the Prodigal Son *represents* God, in the same way as the Good Shepherd of John $10^{1ff.}$ not only represents, but is, Jesus. The first two are

[19] Other possible reminiscences occur in the narrative of the end of Judas Iscariot in Acts 1^{18} (where we should read 'swollen' for 'headlong'), Luke $12^{47f.}$; 1 Corinthians 1^{27}, the story of the Prodigal Son (see below), and a quotation in 2 Peter 2^{22}.

parables, though Luke does not call them so; the 'Good Shepherd' is an *allegory*. Reaping 'where I did not sow', gathering 'where I did not scatter' (which might be translated 'expecting large returns for little or no outlay') would never, by any evangelist, have been put upon the lips of Jesus, if he thought He was speaking directly of Himself. All the same, whether Jesus is really a hard Master or not, it remains true that we must risk our souls to save them,[20] even though our souls are not really ours to risk. 'What shall it profit a man if he gain the whole world, and lose his soul?' Yet we must lose our souls if we are to save them.

We noticed, when dealing with the parable of the Pounds (Luke 19[11ff.]), that the successful slaves receive *unequal* rewards in Luke, and an equal commendation in the First Gospel. That all who have done their best come out equal in the long run, and that (though there are to be many strange changes of position in the eventful history of the pilgrim's progress) at the end of it all it will be found that the words 'first' and 'last', have no longer any meaning, is clear also from the story of the Labourers in the Vineyard. All who 'endure to the end' are to get home in the long run, but some have farther to go than others, because they, too, must 'learn utterly to despair of themselves, and of all else but Christ'. And to get home is not to rule ten or five cities, but to hear the words, 'Enter into the joy of thy Lord', a joy we share equally with all the others, or not at all.

[20] The best-attested of all the sayings of Jesus.

CHAPTER SIX

LUCAN STORIES NOT CALLED 'PARABLES'

In this chapter we are concerned with stories told by Jesus in Luke's Gospel. Luke does not say they were parables, but some of them have all the marks of the parable-type, the elements of risk and surprise being very much to the fore in them. They are the Creditor and his two Debtors ($7^{41ff.}$), the Good Samaritan ($10^{30ff.}$), the Importunate Neighbour ($11^{5ff.}$), the Rich Man's Supper ($14^{16ff.}$), the Woman and her Lost Coin ($15^{8ff.}$), the Prodigal Son ($15^{11ff.}$), the Unjust Steward ($16^{ff.1}$), the Rich Man and Lazarus ($16^{19ff.}$), and the Pharisee and the Publican ($18^{9ff.}$).

It is characteristic of some of these stories that they have a kind of twist in them. A good example of this peculiarity can be found in the story of a creditor who forgave both of his debtors (though one owed him a large sum, and the other a comparatively small sum of money), embedded in the narrative of the woman who washed the Lord's feet with her tears and dried with her hair at Simon the Pharisee's house. Did the woman love much because she was forgiven much, or was she forgiven much because her behaviour showed how much she loved? The story of the creditor and his debtors suggests the former, and so do the last words in 7^{47} ('to whom little was forgiven, the same loves little'). On the other hand, the words 'I tell you, her sins, which are many, are forgiven because she loved much' could naturally be taken to mean 'she was forgiven because she loved', and this interpretation seems to be confirmed by verse 50 ('And he said to the woman, Thy faith has saved thee; go in peace'). It is possible to interpret verse 47 as meaning 'Inasmuch as she loved much, I tell you that her many sins have been forgiven', but this can only be done by an unnatural twist of the text. The 'Western' text evades the difficulty by reading in verse 47, 'I tell you much has been forgiven her', omitting the rest of the verse ('because she loved much', etc.). This is one way of cutting the knot but, if it is accepted, what becomes of the story of the creditor and his two debtors? The real question is: 'When was the woman forgiven?' Had she met Jesus *before* she came to Simon's house, and did she pour out her heart at His feet *because* she had been so greatly forgiven? If so, verses 48–50 are unnecessary, unless they were meant as a confirmation, purely for Simon's benefit, of the fact that the woman whom he had condemned out of hand had already been reclaimed. On the whole, the difficulty of making the story told by Jesus fit the story told by Luke is so great that some expositors have been forced to the conclusion that they were originally separate, and were brought together by the evangelist.[1] Possibly they are right, for the idea that the debtor who is forgiven most always loves most seems somewhat precarious, and the further implication that the woman was a great sinner, and Simon with his lack of love or even common courtesy a little one, seems artificial. Personally, I should like the story to mean that the woman's loving spirit atoned for her sin,[2] but then I have no business to impose what may very well be romantic ideas of my own upon the text. A high note is, after all, struck by 'He graciously forgave them both' solely because they had 'nothing to pay'. Here is the gospel—a veritable 'bolt from the blue' for Simon the Pharisee; loving and unloving are both forgiven, whether they recognize the fact or not. God's forgiveness is as free as the sunshine and the air, and as independent of man's appreciation as they. Of course, all the sunshine and air in the world do not benefit a man if he chooses to lock himself up in an airtight chamber and turn on the gas. And that is what the censorious, self-satisfied, unforgiving Simons of the world are doing. They will not come out into the sunshine, because they are afraid of giving themselves away; they prefer their darkened rooms with their reputation or their grievances for company. I am fairly sure that something like this is what the passage as a whole means, but am inclined to think that there has been some confusion in the tradition, possibly just because the gospel in it is so shattering to our human pretensions and conventional classifications.

In the story of the Good Samaritan—surely a parable, if ever there was one, though Luke does not call it so—there is also a kind of twist. The parables of Jesus are seldom so straightforward as a cursory reading would suggest. In this case the 'twist' is not due to any confusion, but lies in the nature of things.

[1] I can find no reference to the story of the creditor and his two debtors in T. W. Manson's *The Sayings of Jesus*: surely this is teaching-matter peculiar to Luke.

[2] On the principle enunciated in James 5^{20}, 1 Peter 4^{8}. ('Love covers most sins.')

The scribe[3] asks, 'Who is my neighbour?'—Jesus does not answer this question, but asks another, 'To whom can I prove myself a neighbour?' (Luke 10³⁶). This fact illustrates the use of all these words denoting personal relations by Jesus (father, son, brother, neighbour, etc.). A father is not a father because he is the head of a family; he is one who behaves like a father. In the same way a son is one who obeys like a son. The question of our Lord's metaphysical relationship to His Father is not in the field of view of the Synoptic Gospels, though the Fourth Gospel may seem (I doubt even this) to be looking in that direction. It really only appeared over the horizon when Greek philosophy came into contact with Christian propaganda. To the Hebrew mind reality is always concrete and is based upon relations between persons interpreted morally. Only a Jew could have said 'God is love', and even when the word 'Truth' is used, the Greek means logical truth or consistency, truth of idea; the Hebrew, trustworthiness; we mean actual fact. So to the Hebrew mind men are 'brothers' only when they behave like brothers, and neighbours when they act in a neighbourly fashion.[4]

Some interpreters have found a difficulty in the idea that a Samaritan could function as a commercial traveller (that is what the words 'as he journeyed' mean) on the road from Jericho to Jerusalem for, as we read elsewhere (John 4^{9}), 'Jews have no dealings with Samaritans'. It has been surmised that the original order was priest, Levite, Israelite (that is, 'layman').[5] There is force in this criticism of the story, if it is really an account of something that had actually happened—as I believe it is—but may not 'Samaritan' here mean 'religious outcast' or 'outsider', as when the Jews say to Jesus (in John 8^{48}) 'Do we not say well of Thee that Thou art a Samaritan and hast a demon?' Clearly they did not mean that He was racially a Samaritan. T. W. Manson suggests[6] with much probability that the so-called 'Good

[3] In Luke's Gospel scribes or Rabbis are often called 'lawyers', though they were not professional lawyers in our sense of the word, because 'Theophilus', to whom the Third Gospel and the Acts of the Apostles were dedicated, being a Gentile, would imagine that a 'scribe' meant a clerk or secretary.

[4] I may be allowed to refer to a little book of mine (*What did Jesus Teach?*) which has been long out of print, for the working out in greater detail of this theme. Perhaps a conclusive proof of their truth, as far as our Lord is concerned, can be found in 'So shall you become *sons* of your heavenly Father (Matthew 5^{45}) and 'Whoever shall do the will of my heavenly Father, the same is my brother', etc. (Mark 3^{35}).

[5] Those who support this view give the same meaning to the word 'Israelite' in John 1^{47}, but are laymen, as contrasted with the clergy, always 'without guile'?

[6] op. cit., p. 262.

Samaritan' was a non-practising Jew, one of the 'people of the land'.

It should be observed that the priest and (perhaps) the Levite were there 'by chance', whereas the commercial traveller was on his rounds, and the fact that he would have his samples with him made it all the more dangerous to linger on the road when there were gangsters about. 'He put him on his own beast' probably means that he had two mules with him, on one of which he was riding, while the other carried his wares. It is also possible that the priest and Levite were afraid of incurring defilement by contact with a corpse; it is true that the priest at any rate was coming *away* from Jerusalem ('was coming *down*'—verse 21), not *toward* the Temple but, in any case, if he had touched a dead body, he would have been incapacitated for some time from carrying out his ritual duties. His sin was that he 'passed by on the other side', that he did not stop to make sure that the man was really dead—he would not take the slightest risk. 'Took care of him' (verse 34) means that the Samaritan sat up all night with the man, and 'on the morrow' suggests that the night seemed long—we might translate 'when *at last* the morning came'. It would be a good thing if those of us who are engaged in the teaching of these stories to children and young people would procure (if it is still procurable) *The Prodigal Son and other Parables shown in Pictures*, by Thomas Derrick.[7] The artist has done a great service to all lovers of the Gospels by modernizing these stories; he has caught their spirit and humour admirably, and I recommend especially his pictures of the Good Samaritan, though it is perhaps a little cruel to represent the priest as a clergyman of the Church of England and the Levite as a Nonconformist deacon! The Samaritan appears as a foxy-looking little Jew with a Ford car; the picture of his sitting up all night in the inn watching his protégé is a masterpiece.

The Friend at Midnight (Luke $11^{5ff.}$—perhaps better called the 'Importunate Neighbour') provides us with a dramatic contrast with the 'Good Samaritan'. If the latter might be described as a story about a man who could not be called a neighbour behaving in a neighbourly fashion, the former is a story of a man who *was* a neighbour—in the conventional meaning of the word—but who could not be called neighbourly! In a previous chapter

[7] Shakespeare Head Press, Oxford.

we saw reason to doubt whether the parable of the Unjust Judge and the Importunate Widow was really, as Luke says it was (18^1), intended to enforce the truth that 'men ought always to pray, and not grow weary'; to some extent the same hesitation comes into my mind with regard to the Importunate Neighbour. Here we have a good example of the danger of treating our Lord's stories about the behaviour of men and women—whether they are 'parables' in the Lucan sense of the word or not—as though they were allegories—that is, treating them as stories put together to enforce a moral or spiritual lesson. The strict application of that method in this case would obviously involve the expositor in grotesque absurdities, e.g. that the man who was unwilling to get up out of bed until he was made to do so sorely against his will, by the fact that the sturdy beggar outside would not stop knocking, is meant to represent God! The only parallel I can think of to such a blasphemous absurdity is the well-known Cambridge story of the undergraduate who, having passed his preliminary examination at the fourth or fifth attempt, had been celebrating, and was found by the police furiously knocking at the Round Church door, his explanation to them being that he had come to thank the Almighty, but unhappily He had sported His oak, and gone to bed![8] We can escape from embarrassing implications of this sort by saying that the meaning is, if you can make a man who is unwilling to leave his bed get up by sheer persistency, how much more readily will God, who is 'more ready to hear than we to ask', answer the prayers of His children! But then it might be objected, if so, where does the need of persistence come in? I think we shall have to fall back on what is, after all, the very natural supposition, that Jesus loved telling stories about people whom He had known, incidents remembered perhaps from His childhood at Nazareth, and that He was *not always anxious to point a moral*. He loved what we call 'character', and felt that the chief lack of much of the pietism of His time—as it is of ours—was that it was unimaginative and humourless, lacking in humanity, spirit, and fire. We need not go to the extreme of imagining the irate householder coming to the window and hurling the loaves at the head of the man below; that would be an unjustifiable modernization, for 'My children are with me

[8] There is a kind of parallel in Elijah's mockery of the prophets of Baal on Mount Carmel (1 Kings 18^{27}).

in bed' implies a one-roomed cottage where the family slept on the floor, not all in one bed, of course, but on mattresses round a central brazier. To get up and go to the door would mean disturbing the whole family, but would not involve much discomfort; they would soon settle down again. Nor would there be any question of dressing, for the peasants sleep in their day-clothes.

But I suspect that the real reason why the 'friend' was unwilling to get up can be found in the words: 'The door is now—and has long been—shut.' The scene is set in a Palestinian village in which there is no movement after dark. Once the lamp is lit, it is kept burning all night,[9] and when the door is shut, it is the rarest thing in the world for one neighbour to pay a call on another, for to open the door after dark gives the unclean spirits, which are supposed to flock into the village at nightfall from the wilderness outside, the chance to get into one of the houses. Every chink by which the light could get out or the night air get in is stopped up. So, after all, the churlish neighbour, like the priest and the Levite, would not take a risk. My dragoman, when I visited the Holy Land in 1925, told me that Jesus is still spoken of as 'the boy who went out walks at night'; where he got this from I have no idea, but, even if, as I suspect, it was invented for my benefit, it was a creditable invention, for it is true that it is only the coming of Jesus into the world that has given men the courage either to walk the roads or sleep in the dark.[10]

If we must find a moral for this story, it should be, I imagine, 'If you must be meek, that is no reason why you should be mild'. Such lines as 'Christian children all should be mild, obedient, good as He' would, if we took them seriously, give an altogether false impression of what our religion is, and they should be relegated, along with most of the old Sunday-school pictures, to the lumber-room. The whole conception of Christianity as represented by these survivals has done very much to deprive it of any relevance to the aspirations of young and eager spirits, and is more responsible than most of us realize for the lack of interest with which it

[9] May not the words 'If the light that is in you be darkness, how great is the darkness', enshrine another childish memory?

[10] Mr. James Neil in *Everyday Life in the Holy Land* tells how a Syrian lady stayed in an English home for some weeks and, when asked what impressed her most about her life in England, replied: 'Your dreadful habit of sleeping in the dark!'

is too often regarded by a generation which, however dull and mechanical the routine of its daily life may be, is in love with the idea of courage and adventure. When we talk about the life of prayer, we lower our voices: when Jesus talked about prayer, He told two stories, one about a man who would not get up out of bed till he was made to, and the other about a magistrate who would not do his obvious duty until a shrewish woman made his life a burden to him! We have actually succeeded in making truth which, in the Gospels is as lively and bracing as the sea-wind, flat and depressing. Jesus never talked about long prayers except to laugh them away, never used, or needed to use, such words as 'spiritual'—which, I suppose, occurs in every other sentence in some of our sermons,[11]—'religion',[12] or 'piety'.[13] These are all great words, and I am not silly enough to mock at them, but the fact remains—and it is significant of much—that Jesus never needed them; I suppose that, when people met Him, they did not need telling what words like 'religion' and 'worship'[14] meant. He called Himself 'meek and lowly in heart', but neither He Himself nor anybody else who knew Him ever called Him 'mild'. It does not matter so much that the picture left in the mind by 'Gentle Jesus, meek and mild'—very suitable in a very little child's hymn—is, to say the least of it, incomplete, but it does seriously matter that though the adolescent may, and often does, think of the teaching he received in Sunday-school with a kind of indulgent affection, he instinctively feels that he has left it behind him since he left the nursery in the old room at home with discarded toys and fairy-books. The Gospels are not fairy-stories, but a commentary on actual life in the workaday world; they are not about knights in armour, heroes and villains, but about the actual doings and sufferings of real people in a real world.

The story of the Rich Man's Supper (Luke $14^{16ff.}$) may well be, as Luke tells us, a specimen of our Lord's table-talk. It is

[11] Paul did: why?

[12] The word 'religion' only occurs once in the New Testament (James 1^{27}). Why only once?

[13] The writer to the Hebrews uses it of Jesus, and surely he (or she?) is right (Hebrews 5^{7}).

[14] Apart from the 'Lord's Prayer' we do not hear of Jesus giving His twelve missionaries any teaching as to the conduct of public worship. I do not think it is much use giving instruction in devotion in general; when young people find Someone to worship they will not need telling how!

described as an unpremeditated retort to a pious platitude introduced into the conversation at the dinner-table by a fellow guest to carry it on to less dangerous ground. Jesus had already brought out into the open the fact that His fellow guests, while keeping up the appearance of courteous behaviour, had really been scheming for the most distinguished places at the table, and had afterwards reminded His host that there were those living near him who needed his hospitality far more than these rich neighbours and kinsfolk of his who were thinking much more of their dignity than his dinner![15] These pointed observations would make both host and guests decidedly uncomfortable, and we all know the socially useful person who is always ready with some *cliché*, at once high-sounding and non-committal, calculated to ease the tension. This is perhaps best accomplished by changing the subject from this world to the other. But Jesus turns on him when this gentleman says, 'How delightful it would be to be asked out to supper in the Kingdom of God', as if to say, 'Are you quite sure, if you were, that you would want to keep your promise when dinner-time came, that you would care either for the company or the menu?' The familiar story of the invited guests who would not come to the banquet in spite of the fact that they had, some time before, accepted the invitation, and the motley company who took their places, follows. It should be noticed that, though the invited guest in Palestine is asked to book the evening (or afternoon) sometimes weeks beforehand, he is not expected to set off to keep his engagement until a servant comes to tell him that dinner is served. We all know how much easier it is to make engagements well beforehand than to keep them when the time comes. The story is told with much gusto and humour; the farmer and the cattle-dealer are polite, though firm in their refusal ('I pray thee, get me excused'), but the much-married man is not even polite ('I *am married to* a wife'—this is, the grammarian tells us, the meaning of the Greek tense

[15] There is a parallel to this in Rabbinic literature which may throw light on this rebuke. A Rabbi condemns the rich because they gave what were called 'charity feasts'; these dinners had originally deserved their name, for the poor living nearby were entertained on these occasions. But, like many institutions in England ('free endowed schools', for instance) they had kept their name, but lost their nature. A celebrity was invited to entertain the guests, and people of social consequence, business associates and so on, were asked to come. But they were still called 'charity dinners'. Possibly Jesus was the celebrity this time, and therefore was expected to start the conversation, while the guests felt themselves compelled by good manners to take His remarks in good part.

here—'and therefore I am not free to come').[16] He may, for all we know, have been going on his honeymoon that very afternoon!

I have discovered that some good people who hear Luke 14⁷⁻²⁴ expounded in this way feel somewhat uneasy about it; as one unusually outspoken lady of gentle manners said to me: 'I don't like to think of Jesus *teasing* people in this way, least of all when He was enjoying someone else's hospitality.' I think there are two things to be said about this—one small, the other great. The small thing is that there were almost certainly no ladies present, and anyone who has seen, as I have, the portentous dignity with which the Oriental male carries himself on these social occasions, will be able to understand and indeed to sympathize with the desire to prick the bubble of such complacency.[17] The great thing should go without saying for Christians; it is that, if we really believe that Jesus is 'God manifest in the flesh', He brings reality with Him, and it is as futile to say that we do not 'like to think of His doing or saying this or that as it is to criticize the social behaviour of the wind or the sea. The same observation must be made when we are faced with the criticism made by sympathetic Jewish critics like Montefiore of the bitter attacks on the scribes in such passages as Matthew 23—they suggest that in this case Jesus broke His own law of love. In reply to this serious charge we are perfectly justified in admitting that there may be some exaggeration in the records or that subsequent controversies between Jews and Christians in Palestine may have coloured the tradition to some extent, but in the last resort we must confess that orthodox Christians and non-Christian Jews cannot be expected to discuss such matters from the same point of view.

[16] The meaning of the Greek verb translated here, 'I am not at liberty to', is important, for it occurs elsewhere in several important passages, one being 1 John 3[9]. There we should translate: 'He is not *at liberty* to sin, because he is born of God.' It does *not* mean that he actually *could not* sin, if he tried! So in Luke 11[7]: 'My children are in bed as I am: I *cannot get up*.' Of course, he *could* get up: what is meant is that he could not *bring himself* to get up! So in Matthew 6[24]: 'You cannot be in bondage to God and to property'—the two devotions are incompatible.

[17] In the so-called 'Western' text of Matthew 20[25ff.] we have a still more piquant version of Luke 14[7ff.]. It runs: 'You should seek to grow from little to great, and then to learn how to be little again. And when you are asked out to dinner, and enter the dining-room, do not settle down in the superior seats. Perhaps someone superior to you in the social scale may arrive and the slave who summoned you to the dinner may say: "Make room for this man; lower down, please"—and you will be covered with shame. But if you settle down in the humbler place, and your social inferior comes in, the slave may say to you, "Can you find room higher up, Sir?"—and that will be (socially) useful to you.'

From *their* point of view Jesus is a man, open to criticism like other men: from ours He is the Truth. In that case, all we can say is not that the Pharisaic scribes were probably a specially corrupt group of ecclesiastical dignitaries, but that all the charges Jesus brought against them might justly be levelled at some members of any religious bureaucracy, and it is well for people like myself, who spend the greater part of their time in teaching religion or administering Church affairs, to sit up and take notice.[18] 'Let him that is without sin amongst' us 'cast the first stone' at the Pharisees.

As I have already noticed, the story of the Woman and her Lost Coin is *not* called a 'parable' by Luke (15[8ff.]), but it is obviously a pendant to the parable of the Lost Sheep. One outstanding difference between the two is the fact that the coin is described as lost *inside* the house, the sheep *outside* the fold, another that the element of risk is absent in the case of the lost coin. I am told that Palestinian Arab women commonly wear ten silver coins in their head-dress; they take the place of wedding-ring and marriage-certificate with us, and to lose one of them is a calamity. How far we can use modern Arab customs to illustrate the Gospels we can never be sure; but at least the fact is interesting, and may be significant. This story is as simple and domestic as that of the Friend at Midnight, and like the other, may well enshrine a memory of our Lord's early days at Nazareth. Perhaps, indeed, it was His way to provide a story which would interest the women in His audience—we think of the mustard-seed and the leaven in the bread, the new patch on old clothes side by side with the new wine and the old skins, the two women at the mill while the two men are in bed,[19] and so on. This poor woman could not rest until she had peered into all the dark corners; even on the brightest day in summer the only light there is in the one room which constitutes the habitable part of the house comes from cracks in the walls or the open door. Lest the missing coin should be hidden behind the door or roll away as she sweeps, she shuts the door. Now the room is darker still, and she must

[18] I have discussed this question at greater length in *The Way, the Truth, and the Life* (pp. 147f.), and only mention the matter again, because, as far as I can tell, little notice has been taken of what I then wrote.

[19] Luke 17[34f], a significant sidelight on Eastern domestic life; compare also the 'five in one family divided, three against two, and two against three' in Luke 12[52f], the men having a difference because the women are at daggers drawn (the women draw in the men, and the mother-in-law holds the balance of power).

light the slipper-lamp, and holding it up in her hand, while she wields the broom with the other, she moves about with feverish eagerness, often putting the lamp down on the floor, and going down on hands and knees to peer into some dark recess. By and by she finds it, of course, in the most unexpected place, and runs into a neighbour's to tell the good news, so that the whole village soon hears of it. For some time there is a buzz of congratulations round the door, as housewife after housewife drops in to pass the time of day and share her joy—the shadow of bad luck, which means so much to the peasant, is lifted from the village. There is not much to talk about in the little place, so the gossips make the most of it, and again and again the story of the frantic search and the unexpected discovery is retold to fresh groups of interested listeners.

It is sad to be lost outside the fold, perhaps more tragic still to be lost *inside* the Church. Lately I have come across several such people, brought up in Church and Sunday-school; in some cases they have been attending services regularly for years, and are desperately anxious for light and reassurance, but only too ready to confess that they have lost their way, and are bewildered by the teaching that is offered them; it is tragic indeed to have the name of Jesus sounding in our ears every week of our lives, yet not to know Him for ourselves; to hear all that we need, and are so eager to have, offered us continually, and yet not to know how to avail ourselves of it. 'Yes, I know perfectly well that this is what I want, but is it really true and, if it is, how can I get it?' In these days we are so eager to reach the outsider that we sometimes forget that the real test of our ministry is 'Can you do much for the people who *do* come to your services?' It is clear that here we have the justification for special missions to the Church, for a kind of spring-cleaning to find the one who is so unobtrusive as to be always unnoticed, though generally 'among those present', and also to make sure that our established Church-members do really know their Saviour for themselves. The fact has often been deplored that, when a popular missioner like the late Gipsy Smith came to a town, and the names and addresses of those who had signed what were called 'decision-cards' were sent to their local ministers, most of them were found to be Church-members already. This surely suggests that we take it for granted that they are converted people because they come to our services regularly.

I have had the privilege in the last year or two to listen to sermons other than my own far more often than for many years before and, as a result of that very heartening experience, have become convinced that preaching is, in its general tone and emphasis, far more evangelical than it was in my boyhood—at least in the Church in which I was brought up—but I think, too, that they are taking too much for granted, preaching at morning and evening services alike excellent Christ-centred sermons, apparently, however, designed to meet the needs of established Christians. If we remark on this, the preacher will probably answer: 'What is the use of making a strong Gospel-appeal when there are hardly any people in the congregation who are not already active Christian workers?' But is it really true that there are no outsiders—outsiders in a specially tragic sense—*inside* the Church, and sometimes busy with good works? The preference for noncommittal hymns like 'Now let us see Thy beauty, Lord' to hymns of definite Christian experience is only another sign that honest people feel more comfortable singing generalities about vague religious sentiments than when they are asked to sing hymns which make them feel uneasy. And, apart from our preaching, ought we not to have periodical sweepings of the house, holding up the lamp of the Gospel like a searchlight, and turning it this way and that, till we have given it a chance to bring out into the light, not of publicity, indeed, but of the sunshine of the love of God in Christ, the shy, self-conscious, and sensitive people who do not find it easy to talk about their souls, but, by haunting our churches, show how much they long for reassurance, however little they can express themselves in words. For they are Christ's sheep, and He knows all His sheep, whether we know them or not, and 'their angels always behold the face of the Father in Heaven', and He has entrusted them to us. Our perennial temptation is to call them 'difficult', and so perhaps they are, but perhaps it is true also that they need Him quite as much as the young people who are so much easier to get on with, and more pleasant to deal with.

The story of the Prodigal Son (Luke 15[11ff.]), unlike that of the Lost Coin, is obviously a parable, for it contains both the elements of risk and surprise. When the father not only welcomed the prodigal home with open arms, but restored him to the position he occupied when he left for the far country—this is what the 'ring for his finger' meant (verse 22)—from the prudential point of view he might be said to have been asking for trouble. What reason was there to suppose that, when his hunger was appeased, and the drudgery of the farm-routine began anew, the prodigal would not want to be off once more? Moreover, there was the risk of antagonizing the dutiful elder brother who had proved himself the mainstay of the home! But we must be careful not to turn a parable into an allegory contrived artfully to illustrate the love of God for the sinner, and contrast it with the scepticism of the Pharisee as to the genuineness of the publican's repentance. This is, we know, the sort of thing that does happen in actual life, and I have little doubt that it had happened not far away from Nazareth, nor is the probability of this having been the case affected by our recognition of the fact that at least two Old Testament stories may have coloured its telling. The story of Esau and Jacob—as a Jewish scholar has observed[20]—is also concerned with a father and two brothers, the younger of whom gets in first, while the elder, whatever his faults, had at least gone out 'to the field' to carry out his father's command, comes in too late (Genesis 27).[21] But a nearer parallel is the story of Jonah, for—if we think of the Jew as the elder brother and the Gentile as the younger—in both stories the younger brother rebels against his father, in both he repents, returns, and is welcomed back; in both the elder brother is angry, and in both the father argues with him in his younger brother's defence. But, strange to say, there are Pharisaic parallels too.[22] One runs: 'A king's son went out into evil courses, and the king sent his guardian after him. "Return, my son," said he. But the son sent him back, saying to his father: "How can I return? I am ashamed." His father sent again, saying: "My son, art thou indeed ashamed to return? *Is it not to thy father that thou returnest?*" ' Dr. Abrahams made the interesting suggestion that this was omitted from the text of the Talmud because its source was recognized.[23] A later Rabbinic version has the story in this form: the son wrote to the father, 'Father, I want to come

[20] Dr. Israel Abrahams, in *Studies in Pharisaism and the Gospels* (First Series), p. 11.

[21] Perhaps the copyist of Codex Bezae saw this point, for he reads in verse 29: 'Thou never gavest me a kid from the goats' (compare Genesis 27[9]: 'Two good kids from the goats').

[22] op. cit., p. 92.

[23] In much the same way the parable of the Sower was introduced at full length into the old romance of Barlaam and Asaphat by its medieval Jewish writer.

home, but have neither the strength nor the money for the journey', and the father wrote back: 'Come as far as you can, my son, and I will come the rest of the way.' This is medieval Judaism at its best, and indeed it is doubtful whether Pharisees of any period would have rejected even a publican if he expressed penitence, *and was willing to do what he could by way of reparation.* In *St. Paul and Judaism*, Montefiore argued with considerable force that Judaism has *never* taught salvation by works, but rather salvation by the mercy of God on the one side and the repentance of the sinner on the other. But is not repentance (along with the effort to make what reparation is possible) really a 'work'? It is not exactly merit, for it is agreed that—

Could my zeal no respite know,
Could my tears for ever flow,
All for sin could not atone;

but it is still 'Come as far as you can, my son'; this is far removed from the Gospel-parable where the prodigal's poor attempt at penitence is smothered in a kiss,[24] and no security for better behaviour in the future is so much as mentioned.[25] This is a 'bolt from the blue' indeed, something unheard of in the history of ethics; indeed, its heavenly audacity overleaps the limits of what ninety-nine out of a hundred sensible Christians think either desirable or right.[26] But the meaning of the story cannot be mistaken. No matter why you come back from the far country, or how long you put off coming, or even how often you come, the mercy of God imposes no period of probation, requires no adequate proof of amendment—for none can be given—so long as you come. One verse in our hymn-books (would that it was in all of them!) hits the mark with inspired precision; it is:

[24] We should alter the punctuation of verses 18 and 21, and read: 'Father, I have sinned to heaven, and in your sight [that is, 'from your point of view'] I am not worthy to be called your son.'

[25] Some anxious moralists will argue that it is implied, but I feel sure that this is one of the cases in which the argument from silence can legitimately be pressed. In the oldest MSS. 'make me as one of your hired men' is dropped in verse 21, though not in verse 19. The prodigal is not allowed to finish his speech with a promise of working his penitence out in labour on the farm! Like the fact that only Luke added the words 'to repentance' to 'I come not to call the righteous, but sinners' to Mark 2[17] (see Luke 5[32]), this is vital to the understanding of the Gospel.

[26] Anyone who doubts this can easily discover its truth for himself. As I heard Dr. T. W. Manson say, the comparison of Mark 2[17] and Luke 5[32] can be used as a test. In my experience a large majority of Christian people prefer Luke 5[32], but they are wrong!

Let not conscience make you linger,
Nor of fitness fondly dream;
All the fitness he requireth
Is to feel your need of Him:
This He gives you;
'Tis the Spirit's rising beam.[27]

We must, as we value our gospel, maintain against all comers that '*All* the fitness He requireth is to feel your need of Him'.

I do not wonder that Joseph Hart, the 'Particular Baptist' preacher in the East End of London, had one of the largest funerals ever seen in Bunhill Fields.[28] In the parable the father cannot do too much to express his delight that the boy who had done his best to reduce him to poverty in his old age had actually deigned to come home; signet-ring and 'first robe' (both signifying that he is heir of what is left of the estate), fatted calf,[29] music and dancing,[30] are, so to speak, heaped up in the attempt to express the father's joy. Of course, it is true that the fatted calf would soon be finished with and the bagpipes put away; the routine of farm-work would be resumed, and very possibly bad times would come for the younger son. He had wasted, not only the money his father had advanced, but his own physical and moral strength in sexual excess,[31] and we may well imagine that he was too tired to sleep, the wanderlust and other lusts as well would stir in his blood again; but when he saw his father's face in the morning he knew he could not go. Indeed, it is not easy to be a Christian, but *it is easy to start.* It is the preacher's business to say: 'Never mind about tomorrow, start tonight: *He'll see you*

[27] For 'make me as one of your hired men' compare (again) 'The Story of Ahikar', and for the humiliation involved in feeding swine, the Rabbinic pronouncement: 'Cursed be he who feeds swine, and he that teaches his sons Greek letters' (a suitable motto for the New Testament tutor in a theological college!).

[28] He also wrote: 'This, this is the God we adore.' What a preacher of the Gospel to the poor he must have been!

[29] According to the Talmud, a calf which was crammed for the table, and kept for some great family celebration; strict injunctions, however, are given that he should have a rest from forcible feeding on the Sabbath Day!

[30] Wyclif translated—I modernize the spelling—'A symphony and a crwd', 'Scottish bagpipes and Welsh harp'! He was right about the first, but wrong about the second. But, of course, the bagpipes are not Scottish, but Palestinian; they were introduced into the British Isles by the returning Crusaders. 'Should Christians dance?' is a burning question in some quarters. The answer is to be found here: 'Yes, if there's anything worth dancing about, and at home (that is, among friends).'

[31] This is the meaning of the word translated 'disorderly living' (see verse 30 and Ephesians 5^{18}).

through.' There are sins a man can never forgive himself for, but even then unavailing remorse is more tolerable at home than in the far country.[32]

But we must not forget that there is something to be said for the elder brother's point of view. Whether he was strictly accurate when he said 'I have never disobeyed a commandment of thine', we may, if we will, take leave to doubt, but no suggestion is made that he had ever been anything but a dutiful son, *and it is true that nothing is ever said to the one who stays at home.* This is one of the tragedies of life in the West as well as the East—who has not encountered cases in which an elder sister has stayed at home, refusing opportunities of escape into a larger life, because she knows that somebody must stay to look after her old parents? They live on, the years go by, and too often, when release does come, the unmarried sister herself is too old and set in her ways to enjoy it, and to be anything but a burden to the next generation. This is the sort of tragedy of real life which preachers commonly ignore in their desire to attract the young; but it is really the middle-aged who still come to our services who need most help: the lives of some of them are a miracle of self-restraint, and few of us have ever a word to say to show that we know what they are going through. *No word of acknowledgement is ever made to the sister who stays at home, and watches her youth slip by and fade away.* If a younger sister who has got married and has children, brings them with her, all the fuss in the world is made of her and them, while the shadows close down on the one who must stay it out to the end. There is, indeed, much to be said for the elder brother and, judging by the way the story is told, I feel sure that Jesus meant us to feel for him, but the answer of the father to his complaint is, after all, decisive. Assuming for the moment that the father was not perfect—that he had taken too much for granted his elder son's devotion, and that the son had a legitimate grievance, was that the night of all nights to mention it? He said, 'Thy son', and the father counters with, 'Thy brother'; is there anything more to be said?

Of course, one cannot help thinking of the things the parable leaves out; what about that other 'Elder Brother' who could say to His Father what in the parable that father said to the elder

[32] The 'husks' were carob pods, regarded as a sweetmeat in my boyhood and called locust beans. But there are sweet carobs and bitter carobs, the latter only used for cattle food. They look alike, but taste very different, as I can testify.

brother: 'Father, all that is Thine is Mine' (John 17[10]), and who certainly 'never disobeyed one commandment' of His Father's? But this kind of comment is perhaps not exposition of the parable itself, any more than the fact that Jesus is called a 'Samaritan' in John 8[48] justifies us in saying that the 'Good Samaritan' represents Jesus; it is an addendum to it, allowable and perhaps necessary for homilectical but not for strictly expository purposes. If—as is the case with the Rich Man and Lazarus, which will be discussed presently—a story was intended as allegory rather than parable, greater liberty of interpretation might perhaps be allowed. When Jesus told parable-stories, He was generally not thinking of Himself and His mission, but of His observations of the work of God in nature and in human life.

When we turn to the story of the Unjust Steward, we are not so sure whether or no we should describe it as a parable—Luke certainly does not do so. That the evangelist was in difficulties with it himself, and perhaps only included it because it appeared in the collection of stories about, and sayings of, Jesus which he had made during his two years in Palestine (probably A.D. 57–9) which we have been taught to call 'L', and he was too conscientious to leave it out, is suggested by the fact that he appends to it not only the comment made by Jesus Himself (which appears perhaps in Luke 16[8], and certainly in verse 9) but two other sayings of the Lord which are certainly authentic (verses 10 and 13), but which have no very obvious bearing on the case of the Unjust Steward. His embarrassment is as evident as has been that of many, if not most, commentators on the parable since his time. If verse 8 is really to be translated, not 'his master praised the steward of injustice', but '*the Lord* praised the steward of injustice', we can well understand the source of Luke's perturbation; it will not really do to have Jesus praising a dishonest man! So acute has been this unease among serious-minded commentators—and how serious-minded commentators are as a class! —that some of them have been driven to taking verse 8 as a question, and translating 'Did the Lord praise the unrighteous steward?' without the slightest justification in the text, ignoring, moreover, the fact that it is followed by 'because the sons of this world are more businesslike than the children of the light'. If we read 'Did the Lord praise the unrighteous steward because the sons of this world are more business-like than the children of the light?' the whole sentence indeed becomes almost intolerably clumsy. And what about the transition to verse 9 ('Make yourselves friends out of the mammon', etc.)? If verse 8 is to be taken as a question it becomes absolutely pointless in front of verse 9, which, if it has any meaning at all, must mean that in this particular at least, we should do well to imitate the steward's conduct. If, on the other hand, we take the traditional translation, 'his master praised the steward', etc., and suggest that verse 8 is a somewhat cynical remark made by the steward's master when he heard of the clever way in which his late employee had got his own back upon him by reducing the rent without his permission, we are faced with the unlikelihood of a master praising a servant who had robbed him; moreover, our Lord's comment (prefaced as it is by a solemn 'I say unto you') becomes almost incomprehensible. It may be objected that the fact that 'I say unto you' comes in for the first time in verse 9 proves that Jesus is speaking, so to say, in His own person, and that 'the lord' of verse 8 must be the steward's master—but this is not convincing, for there are many examples of 'I say unto you' coming in the middle of words of Jesus (see, for instance, Matthew 5^{44}). Moreover, it is characteristic of Luke to use 'the Lord' instead of the name 'Jesus' in narrative, the only other case of this usage in the Gospels being in John 4^{1}.[33]

We seem to be left with two alternatives: either Jesus praised a man for cheating his master, or the master he had robbed praised him—neither of these seems likely. Shall we try another approach to the whole problem? There are one or two suggestions in the story that the steward had *not* actually robbed his master. One is a word used in verse 1 and translated in our versions 'was accused', but which really means 'was informed against'. The man whom the Romans called a 'delator', and we should call a 'common informer', was a sinister figure in the Empire, and especially in its Eastern provinces; he made an unsavoury living by working his way into an official's confidence, and then reporting the information he had got possession of in

[33] I suggested in my commentary on Luke's Gospel (S.C.M.), that this use is perhaps a sign that Luke is reproducing stories he had heard by word of mouth from disciples of Jesus like Mnason (Acts 21^{16}); in other words, when primitive Christians were *writing* about Jesus, they called Him 'Jesus'; when they were talking about Him, they called Him 'the Lord' or, more probably, 'our Lord' ('Maran'); (see Luke $7^{13, 19}$, $10^{1, 39-41}$, 11^{39}, 16^{8}, $17^{5f.}$, 22^{61}). For the fact that they called Him 'Maran' when *speaking* of Him, see Luke 19^{31}.

this way to higher authorities. As several commentators have pointed out, the question is thus left open as to whether the steward was guilty of cheating his master or not; the word quite often means 'to accuse *falsely*'. To this it may be objected that he is repeatedly called 'the steward of injustice'. All we can say in reply to this is that, if you are going to insist that 'steward of injustice' necessarily means 'dishonest steward', you will have to make 'unrighteous mammon' mean 'money dishonestly made' in verse 9, and commit Jesus to the truly appalling proposition that there is no harm in making money by dishonourable means, if you take care to use it in making friends! That would be a justification for the people who have tried to atone for a lifetime of sharp practice by leaving some of their ill-gotten money to the Church!

No! We shall evidently have to think again. The steward was a 'steward of injustice', not because he was a conspicuously dishonest man, but because, from the very nature of his office, he was involved in a corrupt system; the 'mammon' he handled so dexterously was 'unrighteous', not because it was money gained by openly fraudulent means, but because the system of which it was the symbol was fundamentally fraudulent. Paul uses the word 'unjust' in much the same way in 1 Corinthians 6^1, where he is dealing with the fact that at Corinth, Church members were bringing lawsuits against one another before secular courts; he would be the very last man to charge all Roman courts with injustice (Romans $13^{1ff.}$ is evidence that he would never dream of doing so), but the system these courts represented was built on unsound foundations like all other institutions outside the Church in this fallen world. That was why the magistrates were appointed by God for the world, not for the Church—Christians should obey the magistrates, because God meant them to live in Corinth; they should not avail themselves of the advantages of the system which these magistrates represented, because God has called them to live 'in Christ'. I have no doubt at all that Jesus would have called the monetary system with which we have to get along in these days 'unjust', but would not either Himself denounce it or make any attempt to alter it, nor would He call upon His disciples to do so. Slavery was perhaps the greatest social curse of those days, and almost half the population of the Roman Empire were slaves; they could be bought and sold in the market, and were almost entirely dependent on the caprices of their masters. Yet there is no sign in the New Testament of any crusade against slavery.[34] If the Church had instigated an uprising of the slave-populations, or succeeded in securing wholesale emancipation, the result would only have been that millions of helpless people would have been left without shelter or food, and complete social chaos would have ensued. I have no doubt that Jesus and Paul both thought any kind of ordered government better than none. Christianity seemed to have little chance of establishing itself in the Roman Empire, as it was—if it had identified itself with social and political revolution, it would have had none. But acquiescence for the time being in a corrupt and inhuman civilization does not mean approving of it—Jesus assumed without argument that the system by which the world was governed then was evil, and yet saw God at work in it, bringing good out of evil.[35]

When we turn to the laws or customs by which the relation between the landlord and his tenant was regulated in those days, we soon discover that they were, like the slave system, perhaps irredeemably unjust. In Halévy's *History of the English People in 1815*, it is shown that the estates of Englishmen in Ireland in the early years of the nineteenth century were managed in almost exactly the same way. Most of them lived in London, and seldom or never visited their Irish estates. 'There were counties in which it was only just possible to scrape together sufficient landed proprietors to form (in Ireland) a grand jury. Without any attachment to the soil, the landlord's one thought was to extract with a minimum of trouble the maximum amount of money from a population as widely separated from themselves as Jamaican negroes from the slave-owners who exploited their labour. Accordingly, they left the management of their estates in the hands of men of business, small local solicitors, "agents" as they were termed.' They were paid not by the master, but by the receipt of a certain percentage of the revenue obtained from the

[34] See A. T. Cadoux, *Jesus and Civil Government*. It should be observed in this connexion that, in the Middle East at any rate, slaves could be members of the household, if not of the family, whereas 'hired men' on the farm were the lowest of the low. In the parable of the Prodigal Son the slaves take part in the family rejoicings, whereas the prodigal, when he wants to humiliate himself, does not say, 'Make a slave of me', but 'Make me as one of thy hired men'. One of the greatest evils of slavery is the consequent degradation of free labour.

[35] Of course, we are citizens of our country, as Jesus and His Galilean followers never were. The possession of a vote and our partially democratic system does make a difference.

rent, which they first assessed and then collected. Clearly they would have no particular interest, in most cases, in the improvement of the estate, and so long as the landlord received his share of the spoils, he would ask no questions. This exploitation of the peasants, especially in the south and west of Ireland, by which whole counties were reduced to abject poverty for the benefit of absentee landlords who knew little and cared less for the country which provided them with their income was, as Halévy shows in scores of pages, filled with examples, the real and substantial source of the perennial Irish grievance—and, indeed, the distressful country has never recovered from it.

In the Roman Empire this system was carried much farther. The right to collect the Imperial taxes was sold to a group of financiers who farmed it out to another group of financiers in the East, who in their turn employed the 'publicans' who are so much to the fore in the Gospels, and each party recouped itself for its trouble by taking what is now called a 'rake-off'. The fact that, in consequence, only a comparatively small part of the revenue thus extracted from provincials ever found its way into the Imperial treasury was perhaps compensated for by the profits of the sale; moreover, payment of tax-collectors was made unnecessary.

It seems probable, then, that this steward was left in sole control of the estate, and fixed the rents of the tenants. At stated intervals he collected them, took his own commission, and sent the balance to the landlord who lived at a distance. When the landlord sent for him, and demanded his accounts, he knew what it meant—dismissal. For though not conspicuously dishonest for a man in his position, he was painfully aware that his accounts would not bear a close investigation; indeed, it is quite possible that he had not kept accounts at all. How was he to live? He was not strong enough to work on the land, and was too proud to live on charity. He might have sought to curry favour with friends of his master, and so induce them to use their influence on his behalf, but in any case that would take time, and it is unlikely that he was in touch with anyone of the sort. Evidently he had not put anything by for such a totally unexpected emergency, and only one possibility was left. He might ingratiate himself with the only people he could get at, the tenants on the estate, and the way to do that—for all such rent-collectors were, of course, intensely unpopular—was to let them know that he was responsible for the reduction of the rent; this he could do by forfeiting his own commission. This was what he did, so parting with a nest-egg which might have been useful to him in his retirement—that is to say, if he could have got it, for the story suggests that they were badly in arrears with the rent—for the sake of making friends who, he calculated, would feel so much obliged to him that they would either find him suitable employment on their farms, or at least hospitality and maintenance until he could get a job for himself.

It will be observed that, granted the obvious abuses which marked the system under which he lived, and which, even if he had wanted to do so, he was not in a position to alter, the only charge that can be reasonably brought against this steward was that he reduced the rent without consultation with the master. This would obviously embarrass the incoming steward and, from a strictly ethical point of view, may not be justified. But it would only do so until a new assessment could be made, and in the meantime, the master did not suffer—indeed, it is possible that he profited by the transaction, for the rent might not have been paid at all if some easement of the tenants' financial position had not been arranged; he probably got his money much more promptly. If we take it that Luke 16[8] should be translated, 'the master [that is, the landlord] praised the steward of injustice', the fact that he got his cash may have had something to do with his praise.[36] In any case, the tenants were relieved considerably, and the only party to the transaction who suffered was the steward himself, precisely at the time when he could least afford such a loss. Of course, we must not rush to the other extreme and think of him as a profiteer turned philanthropist all of a sudden. For all we know he may have been as sly a rascal as the commentators, almost to a man, call him, though—as I have already observed—the original Greek leaves it an open question whether his dismissal was justified.

However that may be, his behaviour was clearly not dictated by pity for the tenants, but by concern for his own future—that,

[36] It is worth mentioning that the old Syriac version, the readings of which we have seen reason to commend several times already, has 'Give me the bill, and he sat down quickly and wrote', etc., instead of 'Receive thy bill, and sit down quickly and write', etc., both in verses 6 and 7 of chapter 16. It is the sender of the invoice, not the receiver, who is at liberty to reduce it!

the story makes perfectly plain. His merit was that he knew that 'no man lives to himself', and, consequently, that a friend you can be reasonably sure of is better worth having than an uncertain sum of money; he was sensible, more sensible than the 'children of the light', people who are only too apt, as Jesus emphasized in the sketch of the Pharisee and Publican at their prayers, to 'despise others'.[37] *There is no such thing as independence possible for human beings either in this world or the next: any idea of living our lives without interference from other people is a dangerous delusion.* Evidently, if the definition of a 'parable' which we have suggested is correct, this cannot be called a parable, but its meaning is as obvious as that of the story told by Jesus in Matthew 18[23ff.]. We are all stewards, not owners of this world's good things (whether these are money, health, leisure, youth, charm, brains, or what not). We are all allowed a commission on these good things for our own use and must, so far as we can, give value for what we receive. We are all unjust stewards, for, firstly, we are involved in an inequitable system by which some get more than they deserve, and some less, and there is bound to be a redistribution, indeed a series of redistributions; the first are becoming last and the last first, and 'clogs to clogs in three generations' has long been a truism. Moreover, none of us could face a strict audit if our accounts were called for tomorrow, for none of us could say he had never spent a penny more, or an hour more, a fragment of health and energy more on himself than he could justify. And, because that is so, we are all 'under notice'. What are we to do? 'Make friends', says Jesus—but what kind of friends? Clearly, if there is to be a redistribution of this world's good things, the friends who can help us most, when the 'unrighteous mammon' fails us, are likely to be those whom we have befriended. It is probable that they will be the only friends we shall find it easy to make, for few of those who are better off than we are likely to be easily accessible. If, as it appears, the tenants of the parable were in arrears with the rent, the steward was the only person in a position to help them out of their difficulty; in a few weeks' time they would be the only people in a position to help him out of his—so they were obviously the right friends for him to make. The meaning of the parable seems to be, then, that in our own

[37] Verses 6 and 7 might suggest that the rent was paid in kind, but what is probably meant is the cash value of a hundred measures of oil and a hundred measures of wheat.

interests before the crash comes, we should hasten to make friends of the people who in the topsy-turvy conditions of this fallen world have become more or less dependent upon us for, unless we come to their rescue, they will go unbefriended. Later on we shall, as time brings its revenges, find ourselves dependent upon them.[38] We are all bound up in the bundle of life together, and take turns at being dependent on one another.

It will be objected by the serious-minded that this is a justification of log-rolling and under-the-counter work of all kinds. One might reply—justifiably, I think—that this is the plain sense of Luke 16^9, and that the critic must prove either that the text is corrupt, or that Luke has put these words on to the lips of Jesus, or agree that, if Jesus said them, the ethic He preached is open to criticism. So far as I know, the only important variations in the early MSS. in this verse are between 'mammon of unrighteousness' and 'unrighteous mammon' and between 'when you fail' and 'when it [the mammon] fails you'. Clearly the ethical difficulty was not felt by the early copyists. That Luke did not invent the words seems to be proved by the fact that he appends no fewer than three other 'morals' to the story; evidently *he* felt about it much as the modern critic does. We are left, then, with the third alternative: the charge of appealing to a low motive must be brought against our Lord Himself—of course that has been done many times, generally in connexion with His promises of rewards to His followers. That battle has been fought and won, and there is perhaps no need to reopen the question.

In regard to the matter of the present discussion, it might be argued that it is at least humbler to be willing to receive as well as to give, and if pride is the root of all evil,[39] and humility the essential Christian virtue—and a very good case can be made for this contention—there is much to be said for an attitude of mind which is aware of the fact that, though it may be now our turn to give to the unprivileged—the poor, the sick, and the lonely—the boot is likely to be on the other foot presently, and we shall have to be content to receive. 'It is more blessed to give than to receive', no doubt—it is at least much pleasanter for some of us. If no one can enter the Kingdom of Heaven until he realizes his

[38] As will be seen presently, the same idea comes out strongly in the allegory of Dives and Lazarus (see, especially, Luke 16^{25}).

[39] 1 Timothy 6^{10} should be translated: 'The love of money is *a* root of all the evils'—a very different thing!

complete dependence upon God, it will, to say the least of it, do us no harm to practise humility in our relations with men. In any case, give and take is the law of life in this world, and Jesus assures us that it will be so in the next. We are all parasites, for we all live on one another.

In the last clause of the verse ('that they may receive you into the eternal *tents*') we meet with a paradox, the sharp edge of which is blunted by our translation: 'eternal tabernacles' or 'habitations'. For the word 'tent' and the word 'eternal' appear to be incompatible. A 'tent' or 'tabernacle', in its very nature, is a temporary shelter; we 'pitch our *moving* tent' each night on our pilgrim march through life; if it were not 'moving' it would be a house or home. Jesus, we read in John 1[14], 'pitched His tent among us' when 'the Word was born as flesh'; the hour soon came in which He must return to His father, whose bosom was His home. The very word 'abide', so common in the Fourth Gospel, means generally to 'stay' or 'tarry for a time' rather than to 'settle down in one place for good and all', and the correlated word translated 'mansions' in John 14[2] means a place where you stay, a home from home along the road. Here and hereafter we shall be travellers, if not in miles, at least in experience; we shall never 'sit down'. The 'many mansions' do not mean many different homes for different people, for 'the Englishman's house is *his* castle' is not a Christian sentiment, but many different lodging-places for the same person. And at every camping-place on our age-long journey we shall be dependent on two things, the grace of God and the love of our human friends.

But here a more serious objection comes from the orthodox evangelical: surely this is preaching salvation by friendliness, not justification by faith; indeed, the text looks suspiciously like meaning 'Make friends . . . because your friends will get you to heaven'. Again, the same argument can be directed against this objector on theological grounds as against the ethical highbrow: if a charge of heresy is to be brought, it must be brought against our Lord Himself, not the expositor. A parallel might be found in the allegory of the Sheep and the Goats (Matthew 25[31ff.]), but that is the First Gospel, not the Third, and I understand the First Gospel is already under suspicion of being tainted with Judaism. Moreover, we can say—and with obvious truth—that the sheep and the goats represent nations, not individuals. But nothing of this kind can be said of Luke 16⁹! T. W. Manson[40] evidently thinks that it would stand more appropriately as the moral of the allegory of Dives and Lazarus, and even suggests that 'they may receive you' means 'God may receive you'. (Compare 'They are asking for you' in Luke 12²⁰.) In that case the comment does not belong to the story of the Unjust Steward, for it was the tenants who were expected to receive him into their homes (verse 16⁴).

The so-called 'parable' of the Rich Man and Lazarus—I prefer to call it an allegory, for reasons already explained—is at once the best commentary on the story of the Unjust Steward, and quite unique in the Gospels. Interesting parallels to it are quoted by T. W. Manson[41] from Egyptian sources and from the Palestinian Talmud.[42] Dr. Manson points out that the story in the Gospel differs from the others in having a prologue (describing the relationships of the two men in this life) and an epilogue (the dialogue between the rich man and Abraham). If we want to know *why* Jesus thought it worth while to use what was evidently a familiar story, we must look at them. When I was in Jerusalem I saw a man in rags lying under the window of a house where a dinner was in progress, and when I asked our dragoman what he was doing there, he said: 'To pick up the bits of bread from the table.' Then he explained that pieces of bread were used by the guests to wipe their fingers after eating; when they were not wanted any longer, guests lying near the window could easily toss them over their shoulders into the street. The poor man—he was not a beggar—was put there in the morning and taken away at night, and managed to subsist on these leavings.

The imagery of the Gospel-story is clearly not meant to give us an accurate picture of conditions in the other world; it is taken from popular, not orthodox,[43] Jewish eschatology. The most illuminating parallel can be found in the Slavonic *Enoch* (often called *2nd Enoch*), dated by Forbes and Charles between A.D. 1 and 50. Enoch is carried to the Third Heaven,[44] which is

[40] *The Sayings of Jesus*, p. 293.
[41] op. cit., p. 297.
[42] See also Creed, *Commentary on St. Luke*, pp. 208f. Both Manson and Creed are quoting from an article by Gressmann.
[43] Not orthodox, because there is no suggestion of an intermediate state preceding the final judgement.
[44] For the Third Heaven, see 2 Corinthians 12², where it is synonymous with Paradise. It is interesting to observe that, by this time, the idea that Sheol (Hades) was underground had been abandoned.

described as a ravine or gorge with two sides, a northern and southern side.[45] On the southern side 'everlasting spring abides and never-withering flowers' (this summarizes the more luscious description of *2nd Enoch*), and there are 'those who' (in this world) 'endure all manner of offence from those who exasperate their souls; on the northern side are those who 'being able to satisfy the hungry, left them to die', along with other criminals. It is described as 'a very terrible place . . . cruel darkness and unillumined gloom, but murky fire constantly flaming aloft, and everywhere there is frost and ice, thirst and shivering', and so on.

We need not go on with the description of tortures, in which the writer revels; the stark simplicity of 'I am in anguish in this flame' is, of course, immeasurably more effective.[46] It should be noticed that there is no suggestion in *2nd Enoch* that the poor and hungry went to Paradise; only that those who left the poor to die were in the Third Heaven, but on the wrong side of the gulf.

Dr. Manson observes truly that the rich man seems to be a portrait of the wealthy Sadducee rather than of any kind of Pharisee, and it is plain that the connexion between Luke $16^{14, 19}$ is quite artificial. The allegory of the Rich Man and Lazarus has far more to do with the story of the Unjust Steward than with the verses which come between (which come from 'Q', whereas Luke $16^{1-9; 19-31}$ come from 'L'). Sadducees professed agnosticism in regard to the future life, and sneered at the popular notions of heaven and hell (compare Mark $12^{18ff.}$ and parallels). Some of them were rich landowners, whereas there is little or no evidence for Luke's statement (16^{14}) that the Pharisees were, any more than the rest of us, 'lovers of money'.[47]

Here we have two men, living side by side with one another, and seeing each other every day; yet there is a great gulf between them, neither knowing nor caring how the other lives. This

[45] Popular eschatology reflects, it will be observed, the kind of scenery with which Palestinians are familiar, the *wadi* with precipitous sides, one of which faces the sun, and is habitable and fruitful, the other wild and barren. It is easy to see and shout across from one side to the other, but not to get across, for there is a 'great gulf' between.

[46] I am not suggesting that *2nd Enoch* is the source of our Lord's imagery, only that the picture given in Dives and Lazarus is a reproduction of ideas of the future life current at that period.

[47] Except Mark 12^{40} (=Luke 20^{47}), it is perhaps significant that the First evangelist, who goes into much greater detail in reporting our Lord's denunciation of the Pharisaic scribes, omits these verses, as well as the story of the widow's mite. What exactly is meant by 'devour widow's houses' is still an open question.

anomaly is so common in everyday life, especially in great cities, that we take it as a matter of course; it is proverbial that one may live in a London suburb and know nothing of the man next door. Rich and poor, employer and employed, especially in these days of vast combines, too often live in different worlds. It is, of course, much less so in country towns and villages, where the notice taken of one's comings and goings is often decidedly embarrassing. I imagine that Jesus, on the other hand, would prefer the often scandalous gossip of the village to the complete indifference of a great city. The rich man is clothed in purple and fine linen (purple above and fine linen beneath) and is 'merry and bright every day' (this is a word for word translation of the original). We must not think of him as altogether inhuman, for it can be said for him that he thought of his five brothers when he himself was in torment; in such circumstances most of us would have enough to think about in our own condition! What did he think about Lazarus, if he ever thought about him at all? His modern counterpart would say: 'I am sorry for the fellow, and should be glad to give a handsome donation to any institution at which these poor creatures could be looked after properly, but why should he be dumped on my doorstep? What do I pay rates for?' Certainly none of us suburbanites would care to have an Eastern pauper camping out on our doorsteps—'he offends more senses than one'. As for the poor man, he must have been beyond caring one way or the other.

By and by both men die; there is a terrible irony in the simple words: 'The rich man died, and *he was buried*.' We can imagine the funeral and (modernizing a little) long obituary notices in the local Press. Lazarus, no doubt, would be thrown into a pauper's grave. That was all the world saw; but Jesus lifts the veil, and we are shown the truth, expressed no doubt in the language of popular eschatology, but reflecting reality all the same. Lazarus is carried by the angels to Abraham's bosom.[48] It is doubtful whether this expression can be taken as synonymous

[48] For angels as guardians of the 'little ones' (a term which, in the Gospels should not be understood as referring only to children, who, indeed, are not noticeably 'humble') see Matthew 18[10]. An attempt has lately been made to translate the '*paidion*' of Mark 9[36] as meaning a servant waiting at the table, but the words 'putting his arms round it' rather suggest a child, and the parallel-story in Mark 10[13ff.] seems to settle the matter. But '*paidion*' can mean 'slave' or 'servant' as well as 'child', and we are probably justified in giving a broad interpretation to the phrase 'little ones' as including all people who cannot be left to look after themselves.

with Paradise; it is probable that it should be compared with Luke 13[16] ('the woman bent double') and 19[9] ('son of Abraham'). The sick woman, the rich publican, and poor Lazarus are all of Jewish birth, and consequently belong to Abraham, and Abraham recognizes all three as his children. 'In Abraham's bosom' means 'in intimate converse with Abraham' (compare 'in the bosom of the Father' in John 1[18]). It is John the Baptist, not Jesus, who speaks airily about God raising up from 'these stones' children to Abraham; Jesus, it is obvious from many passages in the Gospels, attached much importance to actual descent from Abraham.

When the veil is lifted we see the same two men, still within sight and sound of each other, but still there is a great gulf between them, though their positions are reversed. The rich man would not cross the gulf then; now Lazarus cannot, according to Abraham, who represents traditional Hebrew eschatology. 'Dives', as we call him, has created his own outer darkness by his lack of natural human compassion for the poor creature who was thrust in his way; he *would not take a hint, even when it was repeated for months, if not years on end.* If someone is thrown in your way, and you are continually meeting one another by what we call undesigned coincidence, God is giving you a hint that the man, woman, or child whom you cannot avoid is bound up with your destiny, and you must do something about it. We have met this idea already in the stories told by Jesus in the Good Samaritan, the Unjust Steward, and here again, still more forcibly; whether there is any vestige of strictly theological significance in it or not, it must have meant much to Jesus, and consequently we ought to take it very seriously. We are told distinctly that we never can tell when we shall need each other, and that certain people are, so to speak, assigned to us; who these people are to be is suggested, not by our own preference or by theirs, but by circumstances which are never really accidental.

Whether we can press the latter part of the story, as some have done, to imply that Jesus believed in fixity after death is another question. I do not believe that 'Abraham' is meant to have the last word on this matter, for the death and resurrection of our Lord Himself have, so to speak, come in between. Perhaps it is not too bold to suggest that we can hear Jesus, as it were, talking to Himself. The reference to the 'five brothers' who have 'Moses and the prophets' is very pointed, and it is perhaps significant that 'Lazarus' (or 'Eleazar') and 'Jesus' mean practically the same thing. As this is an allegory, and not an objective narration of something that had happened in actual life in this world before the story was told—this is rendered probable by the fact that a name is given to one of the characters, and that half the story describes a scene on the other side of the grave—we are free to see a symbolic value in the name chosen. In a parable proper some selected happening in nature or human life is set alongside of some aspect of eternal reality (that is, some truth independent of time and space), and compared with it, in order to show how the one illustrates the other; in an allegory, eternal truth is embodied in a tale, and therefore names can be *given* to the characters, the importance of which does not consist in the fact that someone actually was called by the name, but that the chosen name suggests the truth which the story is designed to convey. An illustration may, of course, be found in an allegory like *Pilgrim's Progress*; it is likely that no one was ever called 'Christian' or 'Hopeful' before the book was written. In the Bible, names tend to be symbolic, but it is interesting to observe that some characters have two names—Jacob and Israel, for instance—Jacob standing for what the man really was, Israel for the meaning of the man's life in the sphere of eternal truth; it is a symbolic, not a parabolic name.[49]

When we realize that the name 'Lazarus'[50] has here a symbolic value, we see that it is quite possible that the fact that it is practically a synonym for Jesus may be of the highest importance for the interpretation of the story in which it appears. Like Lazarus, Jesus was an outcast from the cradle to the grave, so far as this world was concerned. There was 'no room' for Him when He was born, He had 'no place to lay His head' while He lived, until at last 'He bowed His head' on that hard pillow, the Cross (Luke 2^{7}, 9^{58}=Matthew 8^{20}, John 19^{30}).[51] The spiritually rich Jewish

[49] 'Symbol' and 'parable' are both Greek words—'symbol' meaning something thrown together, and so blended with; 'parable', something thrown alongside and so compared or contrasted.

[50] It is true that there was, according to the Fourth Gospel, an actual historical character called 'Lazarus', but it is likely that the name is given to him, as the name Israel to Jacob, because he was the man 'who went to them from the dead'. In other words, it is suggested by the story of 'Dives and Lazarus'. His actual name may have been quite different.

[51] Luke 9^{58}=Matthew 8^{20}: 'The Son of Man has not where to lay His head' comes from 'Q', and it is clear that the Fourth evangelist used 'Q'; so there is every reason to think that he inserted the words 'He bowed His Head' into John 19^{30} with the

Church which possessed 'Moses and the prophets' had no use for Him; He was a stranger all His days, though He, too, was a 'son of Abraham'. Soon He would die and be buried in a borrowed grave. The generation to which He came would pass over, too; could He reach them from the other side? He had no fears for Himself yet, for even on the Cross He could still say to a fellow outcast (see Luke 22^{37}, 23^{43}): 'Today you will be with Me in Paradise'—what of them? Could He reach them, passing from one side to the other? Could He come back again to those they had left behind? The Cross answers one question, Easter Day the other. The Cross answers one question for, if He is now where Lazarus was in this world, by and by He came to be where Dives was in the other: He too said, 'I thirst' (John 19^{28}), and there was no one to come to His aid. The clause in the Creed, 'He descended into hell' is, of course, misleading in Old English, for 'hell' means simply Hades, the other world. But in a deeper sense it is not misleading, for the salvation of lost souls depends upon God being with us, wherever we may be. We must not explain away 'My God, My God, why hast Thou forsaken Me?', for the redemption of this tragic world and of all lost souls who have ever lived in it cannot be accomplished, if there is any region to which God in Jesus cannot come. And if it be objected that the despair of Jesus lasted but for a moment, we can only reply that heartbreak is not to be measured by time; but we are in the Holy of Holies here, and therefore 'silence is best'. We dare not, indeed, in the nature of the case we cannot, pry any further into such mysteries. It is enough that we know that His name is 'Immanuel', which means 'God with us', and that He saves us and has redeemed the world by *just being* wherever we are, or might ever come to be, for He is God, even when He must cry: 'My God, My God, why hast Thou forsaken Me?' This is a great mystery which no man can utter, but it is none the less true for that.

And, after that, having 'descended into hell', He came back to this world, as one 'risen from the dead'; though as far as this world is concerned, Abraham's pessimism is still unconfuted, we may trust that 'every tongue shall confess Him'. But we live 'by

'Q' saying in his mind. At last our Lord could relax, but it was only on the Cross! The symbolic interpretation of historical details is characteristic of the Fourth Gospel (compare John $2^{9, 11}$, 4^{18}, 6^{21}, 12^{30}, 19^{35}). This does not mean, as some have thought that the details are not historical!

faith and not by sight', and after nearly two thousand years, not yet do we see 'all things subject to Him'—far from it indeed! But we see Jesus, and we know that He is still and ever will be, 'God with us all the days', to whatever consummation the long history of mankind shall reach. In any case, He is now 'bound up in the bundle of life' with the race He came to save, and there is an '*x*' to be reckoned with, an incalculable factor in the equation of moral cause and effect. By the death and resurrection of the Son of God we may believe that the great gulf has been bridged and crossed both ways.

The story of the Pharisee and the publican at prayer (Luke 18[9ff.]) carries the same principle—that no man lives to himself—into the life of devotion. Like the great saying of Matthew 5[23f.] ('If you bring your gift to the altar, and there you remember that your brother—that is, fellow Church-member—has anything against you, leave your gift there before the altar, and go home, first settle the matter with your brother, then come and offer your gift'), the story—which may, of course, be taken from actual life—brings out the fact that our relations with God and our attitude to our fellow-men are interlocked; because the Pharisee despised the other man who, like himself, had come up to the Temple to pray, his prayer was no prayer at all. Dr. Manson points out that three alternative translations of the first part of verse 11 are possible; they are (*a*) 'The Pharisee stood and prayed thus with himself', (*b*) 'The Pharisee stood and prayed thus', (*c*) 'The Pharisee stood by himself and prayed thus'. He prefers[52] the third alternative, thinking that it 'adds colour to the story', whereas the first is mere 'conventional detail' and the second 'contributes nothing'. But does (*a*) really provide only conventional detail? May not its point be that the Pharisee was repeating a liturgical prayer aloud—people said their prayers aloud in those days—while Jesus reports what he was saying *to himself*. If you know the liturgy well, it is easy to be thinking of something else when you repeat it. We may surmise that his spoken prayer was: 'My God, I thank Thee that I was not born a Greek, but a Jew, not a slave but free, not a woman, but a man.'[53]

[52] *The Sayings of Jesus*, p. 310.

[53] A prayer which Paul the Pharisee came to contradict clause by clause in Galatians 3[28]. Something has happened to a man who can contradict his first prayer clause by clause!

The catalogue of his religious accomplishments is certainly impressive—fasts are never obligatory in Judaism except on the Day of Atonement. Bi-weekly fasts (on Monday and Thursday) were purely voluntary, and were generally confined to the autumn. To give tithes of *all* he possessed was to go beyond the letter of the law. As Dr. Manson says, the Pharisee and the publican have nowadays changed places; as someone has said (I think Dr. W. R. Maltby) that the modern Pharisee says: 'I thank God I am not like some people I know, nor even as this Plymouth Brother!' My mother used to go on Sunday evenings to the Leeds Town Hall Jail to talk to the women who had been taken there by the police on the charge of being 'drunk and disorderly'; she scarcely ever found one who thought her unhappy predicament was her own fault. They were, she told me, 'the most self-righteous people it had ever been her lot to meet'! So far as we know, Jesus had not to meet Pharisaic publicans, or perhaps He *did*! We can only wonder what were His reactions to them! Two things, and two things only, take all the virtue out of prayer; one is self-satisfaction, and the other its twin-sister, contempt for people unlike ourselves. The Pharisees were really good people, not only highly moral, but perhaps the most religious people who ever lived; all sorts of good things could be said of them, but alas! they were dead; dead because they had stopped growing. The Pharisee glories in his isolation, while the publican feels his friendlessness intensely—'God,' he cries, 'be friends with me, the outcast.' The last part of verse 14 is 'a floating saying' of great importance, indeed, but contributing little or nothing here. It has been dealt with in an earlier chapter. (See Luke 14[11].)

All these Lucan stories have one idea in common. It can be expressed most compactly by quoting Romans 14[7] ('For no one of us lives to himself, and no one dies to himself'). It is perhaps not an accident that the rich fool says 'within himself'; the unjust steward said 'within himself'; the prodigal son 'comes to himself, and says'; the unjust judge says 'within himself'; and the Pharisee prays 'within himself'.[54] This will probably be generally explained as a Lucan attempt to reproduce in Greek an Aramaic idiom; in any case the stories we have discussed in this chapter might be called, from one point of view, studies in soliloquy. The

[54] Compare also Luke 7[39] (of Simon the Pharisee).

difference between the characters consists not in the fact that some are bad and some are good, but that some take pride in isolation, while others are eager for human contacts, and feel the pull of human brotherhood. In the story of the Good Samaritan, priest and Levite pass by on the other side, while the outcast Samaritan, when he sees this stranger lying on the road, 'felt a pull at his heart' and, acting on his impulse at great personal risk, earned the great human name of 'neighbour'. Another man will not get up until he is made to, though it is his friend who comes to him at midnight, while yet another's idea of enjoyment is to be merry by himself, as if any human being could! Others think their private affairs more important then their social obligations, and in the parable of the Prodigal Son, the elder brother will have nothing to do with the prodigal, speaking of him to his father as 'this son of *yours*, who has devoured all you had to live on, with harlots'. In the parable of the Lost Coin this note is not so prominent, but it is there, as we watch the 'friends and neighbours' sympathizing with the poor woman in a loss which meant so much to her. In the whole of Luke 15 we realize as we read that 'joy in heaven' is shared joy, 'joy in heaven' (verse 7) passing into 'joy in the presence of the angels' (verse 10)—the angels looking on and watching the happiness of God—and finally into merriment, in which God and man share together. The unjust steward in his extremity is wise enough to make friends; because Dives felt no pull at his heart when he saw Lazarus in his misery, the time came when desiring—too late—to make friends, he found himself forlorn. In the unjust judge we have the picture of a man who not only did not fear God, but also 'took no heed of man', and we see how the fortress of his carefully cultivated dignity was readily broken into, while the Pharisee could not pray to any purpose because he despised the only other man in Church with him.

CHAPTER SEVEN

MORE PARABOLIC MATERIAL

IN THIS chapter we are concerned with a rich vein of figurative material to be found in the Synoptic Gospels. If it had been left without notice, our survey would have been incomplete, yet it is difficult to bring much of it under any comprehensive title, for we are dealing now with the ore from which the finished products we have learnt to call 'parables' were fashioned. Some of these analogies or illustrations may be called 'border-line cases', others are only included because they enhance our appreciation of the richly imaginative use Jesus made of the life which He saw going on round Him.

The most obvious of these 'border-line cases' is waiting to be dealt with at the end of the 'Sermon on the Mount' or 'the Level Place' (Matthew $7^{24ff.}$=Luke $6^{47ff.}$). Here the differences between the First and Third Gospels are specially interesting, because their imagery implies different topographical settings. In the First Gospel the 'rivers' are said to have 'come', whereas in the Third the 'river broke upon' the house. In other words, in the former the 'rivers' are not there at all till the day of reckoning, in the latter the river is flowing the whole year round, but breaks its banks under the pressure of the rainy season. Luke is clearly thinking of a broad river like the Orontes at Syrian Antioch, where it was the custom of the well-to-do inhabitants to erect summer-villas in the river-valley, the purpose being to get the benefit of the sheltered position and the alluvial soil of the river-valley, and get out before the winter rains set in. A missionary who had returned from India told me how he arrived in Bengal at the time when the Hoogli was rising, and would never forget crossing railway viaducts over the river, and watching all kinds of shanties in which the cultivators of the valley had lived during the summer racing down the stream to sea! They had been built 'without a foundation' in the soft soil of the river-bed, because it was not worth the builder's while to 'go deep'; they were only summer-houses. In such circumstances, everything depends on getting out in the nick of time. It is clear that the imagery of Luke's version is coloured by the country from which he himself came.[1]

The First evangelist's version, truer to Palestinian (as distinct from Syrian) conditions as it is, is even more vivid and dramatic. Here we are concerned, not with a wide river-valley with—in summer—a narrow stream running through it, but with a *wadi* of the type familiar to visitors to the Holy Land, a waterless ravine with steep sides. The best soil for building and cultivation alike is probably to be found near the bottom of the *wadi*; it is possible there to go down far enough to lay proper foundations for a substantial house; moreover, the site is sheltered from the winds of winter. Nothing is said in the First Gospel, it will be observed, about the foolish builder failing to lay a foundation; his trouble is wasted, not because he built badly, but because he chose the wrong site. For possibly three hundred and sixty-four days of the year his choice might seem to be justified, but it is precisely the one day which counts, for all his careful planning counts for less than nothing when the frost finally breaks in the hills and the water comes down.

In our country we possess moorland plateaux which store up the autumn and winter rains in natural reservoirs, and distribute their supplies over the lowlands by natural channels and in instalments. In Western Palestine south of Carmel, there are no rivers at all except on one or two days in the year when what the First evangelist calls 'the rivers'—raging torrents carrying all before them—come and go. Moreover, the hills are not natural reservoirs; there is no heather on them, and the tops are bare and pointed. The snow lies in crevices and drifts; when the spring thaw sets in sharply, snow and ice melt and everything comes down at once. Till that time comes, the man who has built his house in the *wadi*-bottom can count upon protection from the worst of the weather, and good crops in his garden.

But, through ignorance or carelessness, he has not noticed the lie of the land. Till the fatal day, there is no sign of danger; occasional rain does not trouble him, and such snow as does fall does not lie long. Trouble comes with the first warm day and

[1] There are substantial reasons for the belief that he was 'Luke of Antioch', one being the fact that, in the earliest official list of books to be included in the New Testament (*The Muratorian Canon*, written in Latin), we find the absurd statement that Luke 'wrote his Gospel *before* the Ascension' ('*ante ascensum*' in Latin); this must, of course, be emended to '*Antiochensis*' (of Antioch). It is simply the mistake of an amanuensis who is writing the manuscript from dictation.

night when, though he is too fast asleep to hear the crashing of dykes and barriers, the sudden rising of the wind wakes him. His lamp is blown out in the gale which shakes the house, as if trying its strength for the final onslaught, and with the wind comes a smothering wave of cold snow-water like a moving wall. Then there is a sudden crash as the walls give way, and the brown flood comes surging through. Perhaps he succeeds in crawling out, bruised and broken by the shattered fragments of his possessions, and scrambles after a desperate struggle in the dark on to a rock which has not been submerged; then he stops to draw breath, and looks down to see the end of everything, and curse his folly. Next morning the floodwater has gone as quickly as it came, but it has done its work,[2] in a week or two, it may be, another foolhardy builder may come and settle down on the same site, and the same pitiable tragedy may be enacted again. How old the stock temptations are! How often they have been exposed and yet they are for ever finding fresh victims![3] The other man chooses to build his house higher up on bleak and barren ground with nothing but a thin layer of soil covering the naked rock. For all but one day of the year he seems to have the worst of the bargain, but he survives to see the rise and fall of house after house in the valley below him.

At first sight it might seem that this straightforward preacher's illustration contradicts the statement made in an earlier chapter to the effect that 'safety first' is never a rule of life recommended by our Lord, for the sensible builder certainly played for safety, while the foolish builder took all the risks. But it should be obvious that faith is one thing and fecklessness quite another. Underlying the father of the prodigal son's venture of faith there lay the reasoned conviction that to get back his son's confidence was worth any risk. Beneath the unjust steward's willingness to dispense with the money he might have had in his possession to face unemployment, lay the calculation that having one or two friends and no money was less undesirable than having a certain amount of money and no friends. Even the shepherd who was ready to risk ninety-nine sheep for the sake of one knew that

[2] Anyone who, like myself, remembers the Louth floods will know that, even in this country, given a certain formation of the terrain, a town may be devastated by a cloudburst in the middle of a summer afternoon.

[3] For a development of the same idea (the destructive agency, however, being in this case fire, not water) see 1 Corinthians $3^{10ff.}$.

he was only balancing the possibility against the certainty of loss; if he left the one sheep to itself, he would certainly lose it; if, on the other hand, he risked the safety of the others, he might not lose any of them.[4] The slave who refused to risk his master's money should have realized that it was not a case of safety versus danger, but a choice of risks, as it always is in this life.

With this story in mind we should take another pair of similes which seem to recommend caution; they are to be found in Luke 14^{28-32} (the tower-builder and the king going into action). This passage has roused keen controversy, the question being: 'Does Jesus mean here that *we* have to count the cost before we decide to become His disciples, or that *He* will count the cost before He enlists us in His service?' In support of the second alternative it is argued that it is not likely that Jesus would compare the would-be disciple to a king—I wonder why not? Surely the king is simply quoted as an illustration of a man in a responsible and dangerous position making a critical decision. Clearly our attitude to this question must be settled, not by any predilection of our own in regard to what our Lord might have said or done, but by the immediate context and, if that does not help us, then by such understanding of the general drift of His teaching as we have been able to acquire.

Here the meaning of the context is reasonably clear: Jesus thinks of Himself as engaged in an undertaking which can only be carried through by using to the utmost all the resources at His disposal. Men who travel with Him must be prepared to be outnumbered by their enemies; must be ready, if need be, to part with all their possessions, to live the life, and perhaps die the death of an outcast.[5] We might then argue that the reason why Jesus used the analogy of a king going into action against an enemy much superior in numbers to his own army, was that He felt Himself unable to ask anyone to join Him (in this forlorn hope) who was not prepared to take the final risk represented in those days by carrying the cross to one's own execution. But this exposition does not harmonize well with the other simile—that of the tower-builder, for *he* risked nothing but mockery, while

[4] I doubt whether, in this case, we can rightly speak of calculation. George Eliot has somewhere said: 'What man or woman would think of comforting a mother of a large family who had lost one of her children by saying, "Never mind, my dear: you have plenty more"?'

[5] This is the meaning of Luke $22^{35\text{ff.}}$; carrying a sword was the mark of the social outcast, the man with a price on his head.

the king was facing the possibility of defeat and ruin. If we identify the tower-builder or the king either with Jesus or His followers we involve ourselves in serious difficulty. Stopping to count the cost before we decided to follow Jesus, we should almost certainly never have taken the plunge at all, and if He had counted the cost before He chose the twelve, He would surely never have numbered Judas Iscariot among them—that is, unless he was chosen for the express purpose of effecting the arrest, which I cannot bring myself to believe![6] We are driven, it seems to me, to take the two illustrations as meaning simply: 'I am like a man building a tower who, if he is wise, will not begin to build until he knows he can see the thing through, like a king going into action with another king who at the moment has forces twice as large as his own at his disposal; if he is wise, he will think twice before he rushes into action. If after consultation with his council of war he decides that he cannot carry the day, he will ask for an armistice. But you may be sure that, inasmuch as I have already committed myself to this business, since I have begun to build my tower, and am now on the way to engage the enemy in Jerusalem, I am going on with the business to the end, and that anyone who wants to go with me must be ready to undergo all hazards with me.' Here it is not a question merely of becoming a disciple of Jesus; it is a question of joining Him in a special undertaking which He did not ask or expect all His disciples to share with Him.[7] '*Now*, if anyone wants to be My disciple'—'*now*' *is the emphatic word.* Jesus had work to do which made a relatively quiet teaching and healing ministry no longer possible; the ninety-nine, the 'weary and heavy-laden' peasants who had come to depend upon Him as the sheep depend on their shepherd must be left for a little while. There is a lost world to be redeemed, and He must take things in their turn;[8] in the days of His flesh, that meant laying aside the others, for a while.[9]

Among such crisis-pronouncements we might include sayings

[6] Jesus, it would seem, accepted all recruits who were ready to accept His conditions of service; He did not go about looking for suitable candidates for the Ministry, much less for born leaders of men. When Peter said, 'Bid me come over the water', He did not say 'You can't', but 'Come' (Matthew 14[29]).

[7] Not the family at Bethany, for instance.

[8] See John 7[6] for the reason why Jesus had to take things in their appointed order, and could not follow His own inclinations (compare also Luke 9[51ff.], John 9[4]).

[9] Possibly the simile of the tower-builder is meant to suggest the defensive aspect of His redemptive work; towers were built then for defence, not architectural ornaments (see Mark 12[1], Luke 13[4]).

on the need for watchfulness, like Luke 12^{39} ('If the master of the house had known at what hour the thief was coming, he would not have allowed his house to be broken into') and Luke $12^{49f.}$ (about bringing fire on the earth). The need for watchfulness is associated with the 'coming of the Son of Man',[10] and 1 Thessalonians 5^{2} suggests that it was interpreted in this way before the Gospels were written (compare also Matthew $24^{42f.}$). However we explain the phrase ('the Coming of the Son of Man', whether we interpret it as referring, when used by Jesus, to the crisis created by the Jewish war with Rome which led to the decisive separation of the old Jewish and the new Catholic Church, or to the final consummation which we have been taught to call 'the Second Coming'), the simile of the householder and the burglar can mean no more—and certainly no less—than that a crisis, on the issue of which the destiny of Church and world alike depends is coming soon, and therefore the utmost vigilance is demanded on the part of all the Lord's followers. If the householder has been warned—as in this instance he has—that an intruder could be expected some time in the course of the night, he has only himself to blame if he is caught napping.

What is true of the householder is also true of his staff of servants. We had better leave Luke $12^{35ff.}$ (in so far as it has not been dealt with already)[11] till we come to the story of the Ten Bridesmaids, because it brings in the wedding-motif,[12] but Mark 13^{34}, the little 'parable of the man at the door', as it has been called, calls for mention here. We should notice, however, that it is not in this case a question of the coming of a burglar, but of the master of the house himself. My conclusion would be that the coming of the 'burglar' refers to the crisis of the Jewish war, the coming of the Master to the final consummation. But the overriding purpose of all these crisis-sayings is the same, to emphasize the need for alert living, not merely letting the time pass by, like the man with the one talent.

Another class of similes less like parables and more like a preacher's illustrations is introduced by some such formula as 'To what shall I liken?' 'What man is there of you?' 'Therefore every scribe . . . shall be like', etc.

[10] Which, however, is omitted by an important group of early MSS.
[11] In Chapter One.
[12] It is possible, however, that the word translated 'wedding' in Luke 12^{36} simply means any kind of feast here, as it does in Luke 14^{8}.

It is not easy to follow the argument in the first of these passages (Matthew $11^{16ff.}$=Luke $7^{31ff.}$). The picture painted in a few vivid strokes is clear enough—some of the children playing charades in the street are in an awkward humour: they want to stand up at sitting-down time and vice versa. When the others want weddings, they are all for funerals. Stressing the details (we are always tempted to try to make things fit our tidy sermon-outlines) we might be inclined to say that John the Baptist and 'the Son of Man' are being contrasted: John being regarded as the typical ascetic and preacher of judgement and Jesus as eating and drinking in all kinds of company, the children who wanted to play at funerals representing John's disciples while Jesus and His new-found friends, the publicans and sinners, are in a convivial mood. But surely, in that case, 'we raised the funeral dirge' should come first, for John came first, both in historical order and in the remainder of the paragraph. Moreover, we still have to answer the question who the children are meant to represent who are described as complaining that their companions will not fall into line when they call the tune? Jesus says 'this generation'. What He clearly means is that both the Baptist and He have a right to complain of 'this generation', not that 'this generation' is complaining. We must translate 'the time we are living in reminds Me of children playing charades. There are two leaders, John and I; each has called for a different kind of act, but we have had to deal with an unmanageable crowd of players who find fault with the suggestions of both of us. John is too gloomy, I and My followers ("the Son of Man") too free and easy'. I have always wondered who are meant by John's critics; not the common people (see Mark 12^{37} and many other passages), nor would the Pharisees be likely to call John too strict, whatever else they said about him. My tentative conclusion would be that they were the Sadducees and (in Galilee) the partisans of Herod Antipas whom Mark calls the 'Herodians'. We must leave the matter there with the observation—which can hardly be repeated too often—that Jesus enjoyed human nature with all its queer ways ('warts and all') for its own sake; He did not value it merely because He could get a neat moral out of it.

When we turn to the comparisons introduced by the words 'What man is there among you?' we come nearer to the parable-idea. If there are some things which normal people in everyday life do[13] which show us some truth about God, if we have eyes to see all that their action implies, there are other things which no decent man or woman *would dream of doing* which help to clear our minds of some false idea about God. 'Is there a man among you', says Jesus, 'who, if his son were to ask him for bread, would present him with a stone?'[14] Or, supposing that he were to ask him for a fish, would offer him a snake? Or, if he were to ask him for an egg, would fob him off with a scorpion? (Matthew 7^9ff.^ and Luke 11^11ff.^ combined.) Here surely we have a reminiscence from our Lord's early days when He was often hungry, and would run to His father or mother[15] and beg for something to eat between meals. There were three good things in the Galilean highland boy's world—bread, fish (a rare treat this, for not many fish from the lake would find their way to Nazareth), and an egg (probably hens would be kept by some of the village people). And there were three bad things—stones,[16] which might, if the boy were small enough, be mistaken for the little hard loaves which were his staple diet, but would break his teeth when he tried to bite them; snakes lying hidden in the long grass which might to childish eyes look like fish; and the scorpion (worst danger of all), which draws its fangs under its hard shell when taking a sun-bath in the crevices of some old wall, but shoots them out if touched by prying fingers. It might seem to us to go without saying that no God whom anyone but a savage could worship could ever be conceived of as playing such stupid tricks on His worshippers; but the very fact that Jesus thought it necessary to say this so emphatically proves, if proof were needed, that educated men, as well as illiterates, have only been too ready to imagine the gods taking pleasure in catching poor mortals napping. We are reminded of the last words of *Tess of the D'Urbervilles*, of Homer's gods who amuse themselves by playing mean little tricks on all but their favourites among mankind, of

[13] For example, the commercial traveller in the story of the Good Samaritan, the father of the prodigal son, the shepherd with his straying sheep, or the owner of the cow which has fallen into a disused well.

[14] The Greek word used here means more than merely 'give'; it is nearer to 'make a present of' in Matthew 7^9f.^; so also Luke 11^9f.^.

[15] We should say 'mother'; Jesus says 'father'. We should remember that it was probably not the mothers, but the fathers who brought their children to Jesus, and sing—if we could bring ourselves to do so—'When *fathers* of Salem their children brought to Jesus'. But alas! it is too often left to the mothers nowadays.

[16] For the association of stones and bread see the Temptation-story. Stones are one of the perennial troubles in Galilean agriculture (see Mark 4^5^); many a Galilean peasant must have wished that he could turn stones into bread.

the 'lying spirit from Yahweh' in the Old Testament which lures men to their doom,[17] or, for the matter of that, of our legal formula, 'An Act of God'. We have only to think of the things ninety-nine out of a hundred parents would or would not do to their children to realize that such notions[18] about God cannot be true, unless 'As flies to wanton boys, are we to the gods; they kill us for their sport'.

Of the same general type are such sayings as 'Neither do men light a lamp and put under the corn-bin' (Matthew 5[15]); 'Do not even the publicans the same?', etc. (Matthew 5[46]); and 'No one sews a patch of undressed cloth on a worn-out garment; if he does so, the new patch on the old garment shrinks and drags the thread away from it, and a worse rent is the result'; along with its companion-saying: 'No one pours new wine into old hard skins' (Mark 2[21f.]). But these passages draw inferences from the behaviour of ordinary people in secular affairs for the guidance of Christians rather than conclusions as to the character of God. In any case, the last two of them are of special importance for those of us who are passionately concerned about the reunion of the Churches. The somewhat crude type of religious expression, represented by the motley crowd of social undesirables who followed Jesus during the earlier part of His Galilean ministry, could not be fitted in to the framework of orthodox Judaism; old and new both had their values, but it was folly to try to mix them. The only result of any well-meant attempt to find a place for them in the decorous worship of the synagogue would have been the development of a worse schism later on. It is clear that we too must abandon the hope of a tidy Church, as long as it is alive and growing; the children of converts may be comparatively easy to absorb in the second generation, but meanwhile, if the Church is still alive and still growing, fresh converts should be coming in, and, if they are really outsiders, and not converts from other denominations, some fresh provision must be made for them in their turn. Over and over again in Church history it has been proved that new life must find fresh forms of expression, and the consequence has been that apparently never-ending

[17] Even in Amos 5[18ff.] the 'Day of Yahweh' is described as follows: 'It is as if a man did flee from a lion, and a bear met him, or fled into his house, and there a serpent bit him.' If such a conception of God and His dealings with men can be found even in the greater prophets of Israel, it is clear that our Lord's assurance was sorely needed.

[18] 'If ye then, being evil', says Jesus. He assumes that we are 'evil', but declares that we are not as bad as all that.

formation of new sects with which the Romans taunt us. Our perennial difficulty is, how are we to keep the unity of the Spirit, which is life—and certainly demands some form of sacramental intercommunion—with a complete absence of that uniformity which is a sure sign of approaching death in every other part of God's creation? It seems to be obvious that, in the Church at least, the note of authority, so much emphasized in some quarters in these days, will have to be muffled; neither in doctrine nor in Church order have we any warrant whatever in the teaching and practice of Jesus for any kind of standardization, however desirable that may seem to the organizers of Church unity.

But for anything like a complete picture of our Lord's teaching on this all-important subject, we ought at this point to look at other sayings of His about the old and the new. They are 'No man who has drunk old wine wants new, for he says, "The old suits me" ' (Luke 5^{39});[19] 'Do not suppose that I came to abolish the Old Testament; I came not to abolish, but to explain' (Matthew 5^{17}); and 'Every scholar who has become a disciple to the Kingdom of Heaven shall be like a man who is a householder, who brings out of his store things new and old' (Matthew 13^{52}). Jesus saw both sides of the question, and was conservative and radical in one. There is a place for the trained scholar in the Kingdom as well as for the social outcast, but the highest place is that of the man who knows how to build bridges between old and new and can, by showing how his new discoveries give meaning to old commandments, help to make the old live again. In this connexion it should be noticed that in one place (Matthew 5^{19}) Jesus says, 'Whoever takes away from the force of one of the least of these commands . . . shall be *called least in the Kingdom of Heaven*', and in another, 'Truly I tell you, there has not risen among men born of women a greater than John the Baptist, but he that is *least in the Kingdom of Heaven* is greater than he' (Matthew $11^{11f.}$). I find it hard to imagine that Jesus means by this to exclude John from the Kingdom of Heaven, and am inclined to think that the words 'He that is comparatively small' (or (?) 'junior') 'in the Kingdom of Heaven' refer to Jesus

[19] This is omitted in the 'Western' text, but it seems likely that the omission is due to Marcion, who pulled Luke's Gospel to pieces in order to get rid, if possible, of any suggestion of the Old Testament in the New; like some modern scholars, he sought to reduce the Gospel to a one-sided Paulinism. The results of his handiwork can be seen in many ancient texts and versions both of Luke's Gospel and the Epistles of Paul.

Himself. At any rate, the rest of the paragraph has to do with the contrast between John and Jesus. If that be so, the 'violent men' who 'snatch at' the Kingdom are publicans and social outcasts generally, and John is 'greatest among those born of women' because, for the time being at least, he succeeded in bridging the gulf between young and old (see Malachi 4^{6}, Luke 1^{17}), while Jesus is, for the moment, 'less than he', though ultimately and in the last analysis, 'greater', because He set 'fathers against sons' and 'sons against fathers', bringing not peace on earth, but division (Luke 12^{53}) by His revolutionary behaviour (compare Matthew 11^{6}: 'I congratulate the man who does not feel himself let down by Me'). The objection likely to be brought against this line of exposition—which has, at least, the merit of making Matthew 11^{7-17} coherent—is that our Lord cannot be thought of as (even parenthetically, so to speak) calling Himself 'least in the Kingdom', but I believe it is based on a misunderstanding of His character; Matthew 12^{18-24} gives us an always necessary reminder that our Lord's humility was an outstanding feature of His perfect character. Apart from this consideration, we may stress the word 'called' in the phrase (Matthew 5^{19}) 'called least'; there are many indications in the Gospels that public opinion, long after the disappearance from the scene of the Baptist, thought of Jesus as his junior colleague, the one who was 'behind' John (Mark 1^{7}, John 1^{30}—in both these passages the Greek preposition translated 'after' means behind in place rather than later in time, for in Mark 1^{17} it is used of our Lord's disciples and their relationship to Him: 'Come ye behind Me'). Since Jesus had submitted to be baptized at the hands of John, it would be perfectly natural for the mass of people who had not heard what John had said about Him to think of Him at first simply as the most eminent of John's converts and disciples, and one cannot imagine that our Lord felt that His dignity was affronted by this mistake.

Several other passages in the Synoptics have been called 'parables' by commentators (Matthew $7^{3f.}$=Luke $6^{41f.}$, Mark $2^{19f.}$,[20] Matthew $7^{13f.}$=Luke $13^{24f.}$, Matthew $12^{44f.}$=Luke $11^{24ff.}$), and we will deal with these more briefly. We have at least as much right to call Matthew $7^{3f.}$=Luke $6^{41f.}$ (the mote and the beam) reminiscence as we had with the loaf, the fish,

[20] The discussion of this passage (on feasting and fasting), along with Luke $12^{35f.}$, is reserved for Chapter Eight, in which I deal with wedding-symbolism.

and the egg; for it is easy to imagine the carpenter's Son running about among flying shavings and getting a splinter in His eye; when one of the workmen took Him on his knees to get it out, He might well, between laughing and crying, exclaim: 'Why, there's a whole beam in your own!' There is an interesting side-light on this passage in a saying attributed to Rabbi Tarpon (second century A.D.). He complained, we are told, that people in his day would not accept reproof; if one said to another, 'Cast the mote out of thine eye', he would answer: 'Cast the beam out of thine own.' This is probably a deliberate criticism of this saying of Jesus, as tending to encourage censoriousness as well as resentment at criticism.

The saying about the broad and narrow ways is apparently a Jewish commonplace; there are partial parallels in the Old Testament (e.g. Jeremiah 21^{8}, Deuteronomy 30^{19}), but in neither of these passages is there any suggestion that the way of life is narrow, and the way to destruction broad. On the other hand, in 2 Esdras (4 Esdras in Charles's *Pseudepigrapha*) $7^{7ff.}$—this book is dated by Canon Box A.D. 100–35—we have a rather closer parallel. It runs: 'There is a builded city which lies on level ground, and it is full of good things; but its entrance is narrow and it lies on the steep, having fire on the right and deep water on the left hand, and so small is the path that it can contain only one man's footstep at once.' The explanation of the allegory is appended to it; it is: 'When Adam sinned, the ways of this world became narrow and painful . . . but the ways of the coming age are broad and safe.' It will be seen that the same general idea is here given a completely different turn; the contrast is not between a right way which is narrow and a wrong way which is broad, but between a present way which is narrow and a future way which is broad. Luke's companion-picture ($13^{24ff.}$) of the narrow door and the hand waving away late-comers from the window is so different from Matthew $7^{13ff.}$ that it is not easy to think of it as coming from the same source ('Q'). It will be convenient to deal with it also in Chapter Eight.

The picture of the haunted house, forsaken by 'the unclean spirit' only to be occupied by seven other spirits worse than itself, ought not to be omitted from any survey of this sort, whether we call it parable or allegory. In one sense it may be said to have been taken from life, if we include in that term popular superstition. The First evangelist mentions a significant detail which, strangely enough, is omitted by Luke (compare Matthew $12^{44f.}$ with Luke $11^{24ff.}$)—the fact, namely, that the house was left 'empty' as well as 'swept' and 'decorated'. Perhaps this detail was taken for granted in 'Q', and the First evangelist added it by way of explanation; it is as well that he did so, for it provides us with the clue to the story.[21] In Palestine no one will, if he can help it, enter an empty house, for empty houses are thought of as inevitably haunted.

The generation of Jewish people to which Jesus came had experienced a real moral and religious reformation when 'all Jerusalem and Judea' flocked to John's preaching, and were baptized in the Jordan confessing their sins. But nothing had taken the place of the demon of pagan vice which had then been violently expelled. The 'seven other spirits' may be said to have been the pride, envy, party spirit, jealousy, fear of shock and change, greed, and love of power which were responsible between them for the crucifixion of Jesus. It is not clear whether the unclean spirit is thought of as coming to live in the house again himself, or whether he was content to leave his friends in the apartments he had found for them; what was too clean for him might suit them very well. If he came back to stay, it may be implied that there had been many relapses; this is, of course, likely enough to have been the case. But it need not have been so; the point may be that John's converts retained their respectability, but that the very fact that they had been saved from one kind of sin rendered them unconscious of the new and more deadly sins which had crept into the vacuum their old vices left behind them. Most of us have heard Church members giving thanks that their lives had been changed, and we have not been able to doubt the reality of their experience; yet, almost before they have left the room in which the meeting had been held, they have shown by their shabby outbursts of jealousy, their insinuations about each other, and their censoriousness, that being truly saved from one kind of sin has left them the easy prey of half a dozen others.

[21] Luke generally, though not invariably, reproduces the text of 'Q', while the First evangelist seeks to convey its meaning (compare Luke's 'poor' with Matthew's 'poor in spirit'; his 'Thy Kingdom come' with Matthew's 'Thy Kingdom come; Thy will be done', etc.; his 'Get thee behind Me, satan' with 'Get thee behind Me, satan: thou art My hindrance' (Matthew 16^{23}).

CHAPTER EIGHT

THE BRIDESMAIDS AND THE TRIAL OF THE NATIONS

WE HAVE still two supremely great stories told by Jesus to consider, both of which find their climaxes in a surprise, but only one of which can be called a parable. The Story of the Bridesmaids is obviously based on actual life, and gives us a classic example of the use by Jesus of marriage-symbolism. There are two figures employed in the New Testament in the attempt to find analogies for the mystery of Christ and His Church, one speaking of the Church as His Bride, the other as His body. In spite of Ephesians 5$^{32f.}$, the latter is Paul's favourite metaphor, while there are signs that the first was preferred by Jesus,[1] and it appears again in the Apocalypse of John. Both imply a living union, but the union of head and body is organic and necessary, that of bridegroom and bride personal and voluntary, and therefore it may perhaps be called more deeply religious.

In regard to our Lord's employment of marriage-symbolism, three other passages should be brought into consideration; they are Mark 2$^{19ff.}$, Luke 12^{36}, and perhaps John 2$^{1ff.}$, granted that the changing of water into wine at a wedding is to be interpreted as an 'acted parable', like (in the Fourth Gospel, at least) the feeding of the five thousand and the washing of the feet. Before we turn to the first of these passages, we should make up our minds whether 'the Bridegroom' is a title for the Messiah or not. The unanimous answer of the experts in these matters appears to be 'No: when Jesus called Himself the bridegroom, He was *not* claiming to be Messiah'. In the Old Testament and in Apocalyptic and Rabbinical literature alike, Yahweh, not the Messiah, is the bridegroom and husband of Israel (see, for example, Hosea 2^{19}, Jeremiah 2^{2}).

'Can the friends of the bridegroom fast while the bridegroom is with them?' (Mark 2^{19}) appears to mean simply that these

[1] Though it is perhaps doubtful whether Jesus Himself is the Bridegroom of Matthew 25$^{1ff.}$.

publican-companions of Jesus who have just been described as following Him about everywhere in the early days of His Galilean ministry (see verse 15) are enjoying the first ecstasy of a new and amazing experience—that of not being cold-shouldered or denounced by a holy man. It would not last long, and all the more for that reason Jesus will not obtrude upon their notice just now the fact which John's disappearances from the scene made obvious enough that Jesus must before long go the way of John and all the prophets (Mark 9^{13}).[2]

We turn then to the reason for the departure of the bridegroom and for His expectation of a speedy return to His bereaved friends, provided by the other passages which also make use of marriage-symbolism. So far we have not drawn upon Johannine material, but the story of the wedding-feast at Cana is interpreted by the evangelist himself parabolically, and it may be useful as giving us a clue to the interpretation of a whole group of sayings. The evangelist, it should be observed, connects this incident, together with the cleansing of the Temple, with the approach of the passover (John 2^{13}). Modern expositions of the story told in John $2^{1ff.}$ have, more often than not, been suggested by the special concerns of the interpreter: the temperance-advocate has tried to dilute the potency of the intoxicating liquor supplied by Jesus for this festive occasion, while those who dislike unnecessary miracles tell us that it teaches[3] us that Jesus approved of weddings, and when gaiety began to flag for lack of stimulus, His delayed coming brought the company to life again. Such observations may or may not be true but, if you had mentioned any of them to the old disciple who wrote the story down, he would surely have said, 'No, my child; you must look again. Cannot you see that He "manifested His glory" when the water became wine, and that is why "His disciples believed in Him"?' We can be sure that, when the Fourth evangelist tells us (as he does, not only here, but in 2^{17}) that 'His disciples believed or remembered something', he means 'I did'. And it really does not matter very much whether he saw it on the day that it happened, or much later, after years of reflection. The 'glory' of Jesus is, in the Fourth Gospel, His

[2] I can see no sufficient reason for doubting whether Mark 2^{20} came from the lips of Jesus.

[3] When will expositors learn that miracles and parables alike are not meant primarily to *teach* us anything, but to show us Someone? Parables are 'signs', as truly as miracles.

Passion. Even 'the glory which I had with Thee before the world was' (John 17[5]) need not be an exception to this generalization, for we have a strikingly similar idea in Revelation 13[8] ('the Lamb slain from the foundation of the world').[4] Whether this is so or not, John 1[14], 12[41], 13[31ff.], and all the passages which mention the 'hour' of Jesus, reinforce this statement. The evangelist who claims—indirectly but unmistakably—to have been an eye-witness of the scene he describes, saw (or came to see later) the mystery of the Passion in the water become wine; the water of the law (see verse 6) had become the wine of the Gospel, because it had been mixed with the blood of Jesus.[5] It may be objected that in this story, at least, Jesus Himself is not the bridegroom, but one of the guests at the wedding. That is true, but it should also be noticed that, on His arrival on the scene, Jesus takes the place of the host as provider of the feast (see verse 10), though only the servants who draw the water know that this was so. (Compare Revelation 3[20], 'I will sup with him, and he with Me', and our Lord's 'breaking the bread' (the host's function) when a *guest at Emmaus*, Luke 24[30].)

The fact that the incident is timed when the Jewish Passover was near is also significant, for that feast had become so intimately bound up with the idea that Yahweh claimed Israel as His bride when He brought His people up out of Egypt, wooed them in the wilderness and married them at Sinai, that marriage-symbolism had come to pervade the whole passover-ritual.[6] This betrothal between Yahweh and Israel was at once symbolized and sealed by the 'blood of the covenant' (Exodus 24[8]). At the Last Supper, Jesus calls the wine in the cup He gave to His disciples to drink, 'the covenant sealed by My blood'; the union between Himself and them is to be cemented by the shedding of His own blood, and so the living water which came down from Heaven with Him is to become wine indeed, water being thought of as at once cleansing and refreshing the body, wine as invigorating the soul (Psalm 104[15]). As He was the life and soul of the

[4] It is true that the Greek word '*doxa*' (glory) is used in a different sense in John 5[44], where it appears to mean much the same thing as our 'character' in the sense of 'testimonial'.

[5] Compare the association of 'water and blood' in 1 John 5[6], and of 'blood and water' in John 19[34f.]. 2 Samuel 23[17] (the story of David and his three mighty men) is also richly suggestive here.

[6] Other less spiritual Semitic ideas may have had a good deal to do with this marriage-symbolism at Passover, but the worth of all such ideas should be estimated not by their origins, but by their ultimate issues.

wedding-party at Cana, and as His companionship was an intoxication of delight to the sinners who ate and drank with Him in Capernaum, for 'the Lord was like the sun shining on the face of the land, and they drank, and were inebriated with the water of immortal life'[7] so by His death the refreshment and invigoration imparted by His mere outward presence is to become 'a spring of living water' 'within' the believer 'springing up into eternal life' (John 4^{14}), water which has become wine, because it is now water and blood, life-giving water and soul-cleansing blood (1 John 1^{7}). By the life-blood of Jesus, moreover, we are not only cleansed from all sin, but we are enabled to 'have fellowship with one another'; one with Him, we become for the first time, one with one another. 'God has made of one blood[8] every race of men', but we are united by a deeper bond, the blood of the Lord (Acts 17^{26}, 20^{28}). Till the days came when Jesus was taken away from His disciples, they could never make for themselves the discovery that He was now to be with them 'all the days', for only then would they know where to look for Him, first in the new strange life in their own souls, and then in each other. So Jesus gave them the water of life, and then became the life-blood of their souls Himself, as He first gave them the bread which came down from Heaven (John 6^{32}), and then became the living bread *within them.*

In the other two passages (Luke 12$^{35ff.}$, Matthew 25$^{1ff.}$) the friends of Jesus are not thought of any longer as His fellow-guests at a feast at which He Himself is or becomes the host, but either as His slaves waiting up to receive Him when He brings His bride to her new home, or as her friends keeping her company till He comes to claim her. The parable of the Bridesmaids (Matthew 25$^{1ff.}$) begins with a picture which is stamped upon my memory because, when we were approaching the gates of a Galilean town, I caught sight of ten maidens gaily clad and playing some kind of musical instrument as they danced along the road in front of our car; when I asked what they were doing, the dragoman told me that they were going to keep the bride company till her bridegroom arrived. I asked him if there was any chance of seeing the wedding, but he shook his head, saying

[7] The 11th Ode of Solomon.

[8] The word 'blood' is omitted here by some texts, which read: 'God made from one (man).'

in effect: 'It might be tonight, or tomorrow night, or in a fortnight's time; nobody ever knows for certain.' Then he went on to explain that one of the great things to do, if you could, at a middle-class wedding among townsfolk in Palestine was to catch the bridal party napping. So the bridegroom comes unexpectedly, and sometimes in the middle of the night; it is true that he is required by public opinion to send a man along the street to shout 'Behold! the bridegroom is coming!', but that may happen any time, so the bridal party have to be ready to go out into the street to meet him whenever he chooses to come.[9] He is, of course, an honoured guest, and therefore it is not etiquette to wait for him to arrive; his hosts must meet him along the street.

Other important points are that no one is allowed in the streets after dark without a lighted lamp, and also that, when the bridegroom has once arrived, and the door has been shut, late-comers to the ceremony are not admitted.[10] For other details[11] not relevant here I must refer the reader to *Everyday Life in the Holy Land.*[12]

As I said in *The Way, the Truth, and the Life* (p. 182), I am not sure whether this parable was originally meant to refer to the mystical preparation of the soul for an encounter with God or—as the evangelist clearly believed—the Second Coming of our Lord (see Matthew 25[13]). My chief reason for inclining to the first of these explanations is that the parable describes not so much the coming of the Lord to us as our summons to meet Him. Moreover, the Rabbis said that Moses 'woke the children of Israel from their sleep (in Egypt) to meet their bridegroom, God, saying "Behold! the Bridegroom comes!"' It is possible, then, that the evangelist is responsible for the eschatological set-

[9] It must be remembered that the bridegroom may be only a boy in his teens, and may never have seen his bride-to-be; she has often been chosen for him by his mother, and love matches are uncommon. The feast at the bridegroom's house often goes on until all the resources of the household are exhausted and the guests literally *have* to fast (Mark 2[20]).

[10] This fact may have affected such a passage as Luke 13[24f.], which should be punctuated: 'Strive to enter . . . shall seek to enter in, when once the master of the house has risen and shut the door in their faces.'

[11] These are rather Arab than Jewish customs in these days, and readers may be inclined to question whether they should be used for Jews in the time of Jesus. But it seems reasonable to suppose that, when the coincidences in the facts as described by Jesus and as they can be witnessed today are so many, the truth may well be that the Jews have outgrown what were once the customs of the country, and the Arabs have not.

[12] James Neil (Society for the Propagation of the Gospel to the Jews).

ting of the parable. 'Be wakeful then, for you know not the day nor the hour' does not fit it very well, for even the sensible bridesmaids did *not* keep awake till the bridegroom came. My suggestion then is that in 'M'-the Jewish-Christian source of the material peculiar to the First Gospel—the parable was mystical rather than eschatological, and that the First evangelist, with his strong Christological interest, has given it its present setting.

At this point I want to emphasize what I believe to be a fact almost completely passed over by commentators and critics: that all the greatest sayings of our Lord on the devotional life in general—I say 'in general', because sayings in the Fourth Gospel are concerned with union with Christ rather than communion with God—are peculiar to 'M'. Such are, 'Blessed are the pure in heart, for they shall see God' (Matthew 5^{8}); 'Thou, when thou prayest, enter into thy secret chamber and, when thou hast shut the door, pray to thy Father who is in secret' (that is, who sees what is hidden from all others, even yourself), 'and thy Father, who sees in secret, shall reward thee' (Matthew 6^{6})—actually the *only explicit instructions for private prayer* in the Gospels! 'Come unto Me, all ye who are weary' (11^{28}) might be called Christocentric rather than purely mystical, if it were not that the 'heavy-laden' are invited rather to *share* than to shoulder the yoke of Jesus which is obedience to the Father's will. The very fact that 'My Father', 'our Father', 'thy Father', are, except for John 20^{17}, peculiar to 'M' should remind us that this grossly undervalued source gives us nearly all the clues we possess to the nature of the teaching which Jesus must have given to His disciples on the cultivation of the life of devotion for its own sake. If this parable is really, as I have suggested, concerned with the devotional life, we should count it, along with the twin-parables of the Hidden Treasure and the Pearl of Great Price, as fresh evidence of the mystical value of 'M'.

There are moments in the life of the soul[13] which are foretastes of the final consummation, when the Bridegroom of every faithful heart's desire comes to claim His own, and for this encounter no more satisfying symbol can be found than that last refuge of romance in a mechanically-minded world—a wedding. For the spectators the affair may be just a spectacle; for the parents of

[13] As *The Way, the Truth, and the Life* seems to be irrevocably out of print—it was twice blitzed and can hardly be expected to survive—I have ventured to reproduce a few sentences from it. I can find no better words to express what I want to say here.

the bride, something rather painful to get over; for the bridesmaids, a chance of wearing pretty clothes. For the lovers who meet at the altar it may carry with it a hundred memories and hopes they cannot share with anyone else, a sacramental consummation of many sacraments. But when God is the Bridegroom many share in the joy of His appearing; each worshipper enjoys his own ecstasy, none more than the other. Yet only those who in the long months or years of waiting have kept the inner flame alive can share the beatific visions when it comes. In the parable all the bridesmaids fell asleep; life went on as usual and, if you had seen them you would not have known the wise from the foolish—yet the difference was plain enough when the great hour came. Some possessed, and others did not, a secret which could not be shared at a moment's notice, or acquired second-hand, nor are any shops ever open at which the hidden life of devotion can be hastily procured when needed. Perhaps there is an allusion, in the reference to the 'oil' in the parable, to the flask of holy oil from which Aaron and his sons and all high-priests and kings during the time of the First Temple, were said to have been anointed. In any case, it represents sacramental grace, grace because it is something which cannot be worked up or caught by contagion from others, or induced by auto-suggestion, but which is stored up in the secret life of devotion in sacrament, for 'except you eat the flesh and drink the blood of the Son of Man, you have no life in yourselves' (John 6[53]). It is sacramental partly because it has little to do with our feelings, but everything with His gift, and partly because what He is doing with us we know not when we receive it, but we shall know afterwards (John 13[7]). It is symbolized in the washing of the disciples' feet; all that *we* have to do is to let Him do what He will with us, to be obedient and submissive, and to be content to wait for understanding. Both wise and foolish bridesmaids were assembled in the bride's house for the same purpose, and both wise and foolish fell asleep before the Bridegroom came, but some were simply putting in the time till He came, engaged, it may be, in various activities, and taking things as they came. They had never realized, or had forgotten, that the bridegroom would come suddenly, and that they must prepare for His coming beforehand.

We have seen that the Passover had come to symbolize the

mystical wedding between God and His people, and B. W. Bacon has shown that the discourses and prayer at the Last Supper (John 14–17) are based upon Jewish passover-prayers, which underlie also the eucharistic liturgy in the *Teaching of the Twelve Apostles*. Here liturgies of thanksgiving offered before and after the meal are combined. First, there is a thanksgiving for the cup—notice that the cup comes *first*, as in Luke 22[17], 1 Corinthians 10[16], but not 1 Corinthians 11[24], Mark 14[22f.]—it begins 'We give Thee thanks for the holy vine of Thy servant David' (see John 15[1]). After this a thanksgiving follows for the broken bread. After the second prayer the table is fenced, and three more prayers follow—the first a thanksgiving for the indwelling of the Holy Name in believers (John 17[11]), the second for spiritual food and wine, and the third a prayer for Church unity or, in other words, the vindication of the Bride of Christ. All this seems to imply that we should accept the 'Western' reading of Matthew 25[1] ('Then shall the Kingdom of Heaven be likened to ten bridesmaids who went out to meet the bridegroom *and his bride*'); what is meant being that the maidens went out to escort the bridegroom to his bride and we should translate 'for the meeting of the bridegroom and the bride'. By His washing of His disciples' feet on the one hand, and on the other by the sacramental gift of His body and His blood, the eleven are being prepared for the vision of God on the Cross. What Jesus was doing for them they did not understand *then*, but they were to know hereafter (John 13[7]). Perhaps the First evangelist was not so wrong after all when he associated the great encounter for which Jesus was preparing them with the final consummation, but the point is that, when Thomas said 'My Lord and my God' little more than a week after the Crucifixion, he was saying more than he knew; when he saw the 'glorious scars' left from the Passion he acknowledged, in the name of all the disciples of Jesus who had been with Him in the days of His flesh that, having been so long with Jesus, they had at last 'seen the Father'.

But, if the Bridegroom was to be revealed sooner than they knew, the vision of the Bride 'without spot or wrinkle or any such thing' is still to appear. Only as we are content to meet with what may be a small band of Christian people of our own denomination in sacramental communion, can we ever hope with the mind's eye to catch a passing glimpse of the 'multitude that no man can number'. Here again we cannot see in the normal activities of Church life what He is doing; Luke tells us (22^{24}), though it seems hardly credible, that the disciples were disputing as to who was the greatest at the table itself, and a cynic might say that the Churches have been doing the same thing ever since. But does anyone doubt that He was, all the time, in spite of themselves, drawing them together, because in the case of all of them except Judas, notwithstanding their behaviour, they were already 'clean because of the words that He had spoken to them' (John 13^{10}, 15^{3})? For the time being they were distracted by difference of opinion; indeed, it seems likely that the presence of Judas was the cause of the discussion about precedence, and that they were all caught in the dispute against their will—but our Lord's companionship with them had not been in vain. They were His little ones, the pure in heart who would see God.[14] And, if we in these days, in our little groups of faithful Christian people, are willing to come to the table of the Lord, and receive the 'Kingdom of God as little children', whether we appreciate the ritual or not He will, as a reward of our obedience, prepare us for the moment when we shall understand what we now see in a riddle with many seeming contradictions, and only by reflected light. Then it will be 'face to face'.

Does anyone believe that the Churches can for ever stay apart, if the life-blood of God, as Jesus told us, is really in our souls? But only as we let Him feed the secret flame of love-longing for the sight of the Bridegroom's face and—what should go with it—longing for the vindication of His bride, the Church, can we be ready for the great moment when we shall wake from the long sleep of life to trim our lanterns and rouse ourselves to the glorious and awful encounter with God. Other things we can do for ourselves, serving the present age, or cultivating habits of devotion; this we cannot do for ourselves, for it is in the means of grace which we do not always understand and certainly cannot fully appreciate but which He has appointed, that He feeds our souls with the bread of life, and makes us ready for His appearing.

In Luke $12^{35f.}$, the figure of the bridegroom is perhaps used

[14] This is what is meant probably by 'Behold an Israelite indeed, in whom there is no guile' (John 1^{47}), for Philo—incorrectly, but happily—takes 'Israelite' as meaning one who sees, or is to see, God (see also John 1^{51}, for that is what 'you shall see Heaven opened' means).

again, but with an entirely different implication. It runs: 'Let your loins be girt and your lanterns burning, and you must be like men who wait for their lord, saying, When will he come back from the wedding?, in order that, when he comes and knocks, they may at once open the door to him.' If we stress the word 'wedding' here—I have mentioned already that the Greek word, when used in the plural as it is here sometimes means simply 'feast'—we shall think of slaves waiting up to be ready to greet bridegroom and bride. The reference to the consummation which we call 'the Second Coming' seems unmistakable here, for it should be noticed that the slaves are not, like the bridesmaids, thought of as attending on the bride, but the bridegroom. Nor are they described as growing drowsy and falling asleep, for the master is away only one night; he has already gone to fetch his bride home,[15] and will be back before morning. Probably, however, we ought not to include this rapid sketch with examples of the use of wedding-symbolism, for the reference to a wedding, even if it exists at all, is quite incidental.

But we cannot help reflecting how utterly we modern Christians are out of our depth, when we come to words like 'you must be like men who wait for their Lord'. 'Let your loins be girt and your lanterns burning' we think we understand, for we have exhortations enough and to spare to be up and doing; but when we come to the rest of the text, our exhortations tend to peter out, for neither those who exhort nor those who suffer exhortation are expecting anything or anybody. Perhaps that is one of the reasons why our exhortations often fall so flat.

The other passage reserved for this chapter is Luke 13[24ff.]. I have pointed out in the previous chapter that it is strikingly different from Matthew 7[13ff.], though scholars are almost unanimous in regarding these two sayings as coming from a common original ('Q'). Not only have we here a door to a house instead of a gate leading to a path, but whereas in the First Gospel the difficulty consists in *finding* the gate, in Luke it consists in forcing one's way in. Many seek to enter in Luke; few even *look* for the

[15] This may be taken as implying that the Second Coming will not be delayed when the Bride (the Church) is ready, but perhaps we should not stress details unduly. Most of us, I suppose, believe that the Second Coming does not really involve a *second* coming, but a recognition by the world of the meaning of the First Coming. This is 'the sign of the Son of Man in Heaven' (Matthew 24[30]), also called 'the revelation of the Son of Man'. He is here already (Matthew 28[20]), but then 'He will be revealed, and every knee shall bow', etc. (Philippians 2[10f.]).

way in the First Gospel. It should be noticed also that, whereas in the corresponding passage in the First Gospel Jesus Himself is described (Matthew 7^{23}) as refusing to acknowledge people who claimed to have done yeoman service in His cause, and by the use of His name, in the words 'I never knew *you*', in Luke the 'Master of the house' denies admittance to people who claim to have 'eaten and drunk in' His 'presence', and listened to His teaching in their streets in the words: '*it does not matter to Me where you come from.*' No matter how much you have done for Me, says Jesus in the First Gospel, no matter how much I have done for you, He says in Luke, it does not follow that you are Mine. From the critical point of view all this is very perplexing; it is not merely that we are confronted with two passages which are almost entirely different in wording, but that their meaning is almost as different as it can be. I am strongly inclined to think that one comes from 'L' (Luke's special material) and the other from 'M'. It is difficult to say which of the two passages is the more intimidating; if the First Gospel gives successful evangelists a stern warning, Luke gives their hearers an equally startling reminder that neither are they secure, for in each case the Lord does not deny that the claim His clients make is justified! Perhaps the only thing we can do is to say with Charles Wesley:

Ah! Lord, with trembling I confess,
A gracious soul may fall from grace;
The salt may lose its seasoning power,
And never, never find it more.

Lest that my fearful case should be,
Each moment knit my soul to Thee;
And lead me to the mount above,
Through the low vale of humble love.

So we come to the last story Jesus told before going to the Cross, and in this case surely no one will call it a parable; it is an allegory or drama of judgement. Probably we should do well not to call it the allegory of the sheep and the goats, for the words, 'as a shepherd divides the sheep and the goats' are merely an incidental metaphor, and the figure is not referred to again. We might call it 'the judgement of the Gentiles', for it is more nearly in a prophetic vein than any other words of Jesus except those addressed to the cities in which most of His mighty works had been done, and to Jerusalem. Two or three preliminary questions must be answered before we attempt its exposition.

As Dr. T. W. Manson points out,[16] the principal characters, apart from the nations (or Gentiles) in the drama, are (1) the 'Son of Man' accompanied by the angels, (2) the King, (3) the King's Father, (4) the King's brethren. By the 'King's Father' is meant God; and so the King must represent Jesus Himself. The difficulty here is that Jesus rarely or never speaks of Himself as a 'king'; God is, generally, the King, and His Kingdom is 'the Kingdom of God', not Jesus. Even when the dying revolutionary says to Jesus on the Cross, 'Lord, remember me when thou comest in Thy kingdom', Jesus only answers: 'Today thou shalt be with Me in Paradise' (not 'in My kingdom'). It is, of course, possible that Jesus thought of Himself as a 'king' for the first time on the eve of His Passion; this would fit in very well with the Johannine idea of the Cross being the 'glory' of Jesus. Moreover, in John 18^{37}, Jesus does mention 'My kingdom' to Pilate, but the whole passage reads not 'I am a king', but 'you say that I am a king'—a very different thing![17]

The King, then, is either identical with Jesus or with a group consisting of Himself and His disciples whom He calls 'Son of Man'. But who are 'the nations'? The fact that everywhere else in the First Gospel the word '*ethnē*' is translated 'Gentiles' (see Matthew 4^{15}, 5^{47} ('*ethnikoi*'); 6^{32}, 10^{5}, $12^{18, 21}$, 18^{17} ('*ethnikos*'); 20^{19}, 21^{43} (possibly 'nation' here, but it seems to mean a Gentile nation), 24^{14}) suggests that the only reason why it has not been translated 'Gentiles' here is the desire to avoid the suggestion that by the 'little brothers' of Jesus may here be meant the Jews. There are three possible interpretations of this last warning to the nations of the world. Either Jesus is calling all sick, distressed or homeless people His little brothers, or His disciples, or His kinsmen the Jews, in those terms. If the first of these three interpretations is accepted, the Gentile nations are to be judged by their treatment of displaced persons, prisoners, and the sick—but why the Gentiles only? The second interpretation is suggested by a comparison with such passages as Mark 9^{41} ('Whoever shall

16 *The Sayings of Jesus*, p. 249.

17 As we have seen, Luke 14^{31} should not count and, though Matthew 20^{21} has 'in Thy kingdom', Mark's Gospel—which gives us the earlier version—has 'in Thy glory'.

give *you* a cup of cold water . . . shall not lose his reward'). All the same, I feel that the very fact that the *Gentiles* are to be judged by this test and that this allegory is the last and perhaps the most solemn of all pictures of judgement uttered by Jesus—indeed, may well be called His final verdict on international history—implies that, to put the matter at its lowest, we ought not to dismiss without consideration (as most commentators do) the possibility that our Lord, knowing only too well what the fate of His people would be (for did He not weep over Jerusalem, and bid the women who mourned for Him as He climbed Golgotha to weep for themselves rather than for Him?), in the last of His great utterances before His passion here commends His doomed people to the compassion of Gentile Christendom, and declares that by their treatment of the wandering Jew they will be judged. Indeed, what could be more natural? We had better not inquire how the charge has been carried out, nor need we boggle at the phrase 'eternal punishment', for the word 'eternal' here means 'lasting from age to age', and has not this been the experience of the nations of Europe ever since? There has not been peace for fifty years together in Europe from the time the warning was uttered! 'Will He not avenge His own elect, who cry to Him day and night? Yes, I say, and speedily!' It is not that God is vengeful, but that there *can be no peace* while Christian gentlemen (like Shakespeare's Antonio) spurn and vilify the people who gave us our Bible and our Saviour, because so many of them have become what we made them—money-lenders and company-promoters, or dealers in old clothes! What other trades could they learn, when for centuries they were not allowed to earn their living in any other way! Whether this allegory is to be interpreted in this way or not—and I find few who will even look at it, though it seems straightforward enough—it is time to say outright that the general tone of Christian society when Jews are being discussed is despicably mean. It is time we mended our manners, to say the least of it.

Whatever we call this narrative, and however it is interpreted, it will be agreed that it shows one of the marks of the true parable; it culminates in an overwhelming surprise. The Gentiles have entertained many ideas of divine kingship, but never this; at last the truth is revealed, and simple human compassion is seen on the throne of the Universe! Neither the nations on the right hand nor the nations on the left had ever dreamed of this, and they are all depicted as unable to believe their eyes. There is only one alteration anyone could wish to make in the text of the First Gospel in these chapters (24, 25). Surely the reckless slave and the over-cautious slave should go into the outer darkness together, as both alike fail to prepare for the coming of the king; and the two narratives—the one describing the secret preparation of the heart and the other the unconscious preparation for the same coming in the outward life of service inspired by compassion—should also go together. There we can leave the matter; all has been said by the Lord that even He could say. Now He passes on to action, for 'the passover is coming, and the Son of Man is to be handed over to be crucified'. He is not merely going to identify Himself, as He has done in word, with the dispossessed of all time—He is to be 'numbered with them' for ever. Truly, as a Polish Jew once said: 'Christianity is *the* religion for all poor devils!'

CHAPTER NINE

GENERAL CONCLUSIONS

We have covered a good deal of ground, and there is perhaps some danger of our not seeing the wood for the trees. One thing we have discovered as we made our way through a complex and perhaps not very conclusive discussion as to the true meaning of the word 'parable' in the Gospels, is that Jesus was intensely interested in the everyday life of the people round Him. Many of the stories He told cannot be said to be obtrusively religious in tone, nor do they in the least resemble selections from the lives of the saints, sometimes indeed it is not easy to distil a theological meaning out of them at all. One of His stories commends a man generally considered by expositors as a decidedly doubtful character, but this is not surprising, for on more than one occasion Jesus praised the behaviour of people who had undoubtedly earned the bad name they got, a scandalous reputation as traitors or harlots. There are certainly no *religious* stories anywhere quite like these. Moreover, what we call the clerical profession tends to play a sorry part in them, and scarcely a single religious person comes off really well. This is all the more remarkable because there are plenty of signs in the Gospels that several important people in the Jewish Church were sympathetic to Jesus, and some of them did their best to help Him in a discreet way, but they do not appear in the parables.

All this is true, and I do not wonder that our opponents enjoy reminding us of it. Nor am I in the least surprised that ecclesiastical dignitaries of our Lord's own time bitterly resented His tone. So should I, if I had been a Rabbi, and did not know who my critic was, if an outsider had come into a lecture of mine, and had said to me in the presence of people who, till he came, seemed to be hanging on my words: 'People like you box the compass to make one convert to your views and, when you have got him, you make him twice as much of a lost soul as you are yourself.'[1] I have occasionally met people afflicted with what I can only call an anti-ministerial complex; I have

[1] Matthew 23¹⁵.

never heard any of them say—whatever they may have thought—anything quite as shattering as this![2] I do not wonder, either, that modern apologists for Judaism complain that, in this passage and in others like it, Jesus broke His own law of love.

Even present-day preachers find it easier to preach from Paul's Epistles than from the Gospel parables, if my experience as a listener to sermons is any guide; and this is natural, for Paul, though of immeasurably greater stature and spiritual genius than any of us was, after all, a man like the rest of us; whereas when Jesus speaks, God is speaking, and we cannot fit His values into ours—which are the result of centuries of Christian tradition—any more than we can contain the marvels of nature in our aesthetic canons and critical appreciations. What Carlyle said to a young lady who told him that she had decided upon mature consideration to 'accept the universe' ('You'd better') is true of the words of Jesus; we have no option but to accept them, though some of us are only deterred from openly expressing our dissatisfaction with several of them by reverence. Of course, this does not mean that we should refuse to pass any kind of critical judgement on the documents which contain them; but it does mean that, if we are convinced that Jesus was 'God manifest in the flesh', and that the evidence that He said such and such things is sufficient to make it probable that they actually passed His lips, we must attach more importance to them than to all the utterances of His most truly inspired followers.

It is often said that the person of Christ Himself is the only absolutely *new* thing He brought with Him into the world, and that a parallel can be found to all the details of His ethical teaching, if not in the Old Testament, then in apocryphal or pseudepigraphic Jewish literature. It is true that there are many such parallels, though they are mixed up with so much other matter that they are difficult to discover for oneself; certainly we could unearth sayings which might be regarded as fairly close parallels to 'Love your enemies', for instance.[3] This ought not to surprise

[2] It was not because they made any kind of living—as I do—out of religion: certainly, whatever may be said of the priests, the Rabbis were not paid for preaching or teaching.

[3] I mention one from the 'Testament of Gad' in the book called *The Testament of the Twelve Patriarchs* (about 100 B.C.). It runs: 'If he [a man] be shameless and persisteth in his wrong-doing, even so forgive him from the heart, and leave to God the avenging.' Charles calls it the most remarkable statement on forgiveness in the whole of ancient literature.

us in the least, for many of us could, without much trouble, join in a competition in idealist utterance. No one would wish to cavil at such expressions of noble thought, and of this example we can only say—we can give its unknown author no higher tribute—that it is not unworthy of the inspired people from which it comes. But this does not touch the fringe of the question: 'In what does the real uniqueness of the *parables* of Jesus consist?' Not surely in their ethical idealism (for anyone, so long as he keeps to generalities, could rival that), but rather to the fact that they are utterly unlike (not in degree so much as in kind) other parabolic literature in the Bible and elsewhere outside the Gospels. It is not the ethical insights that can be distilled from His parables that are unique, but the gospel contained in or suggested by them.

It would be worth while to take the Galilean miracles into our purview as we try to explain what this statement means. We must, by an effort of imagination, put ourselves back into the atmosphere of those halcyon days when, in spite of mutterings in the background from shocked ecclesiastics and indignant moralists hobnobbing with uneasy politicians (Mark 3^{6}), the friends of Jesus simply could not be overawed, or made to fast.[4] 'Who is this?' the disciples say—He scolds the winds and the waves on the lake as though they were tiresome children,[5] and His slightest word sends demons scurrying for dear life back to the abyss from which they came. Power streams from His very clothes, and the poor crazed Gerasene, like a child who has waked shivering and trembling from a long nightmare, clings to Him and begs to be allowed to stay with Him, safe from the fears which had driven him mad, as long as he can hold His hand, while Jairus's little daughter comes out of the strange borderland between life and death when he calls her by her pet-name. 'These men were full of new wine,' for here was something new, explosive like the yeast in the dough and, like a dragnet in the sea, with an irresistible attraction for all kinds of queer human fish. Before long other moods express themselves in another kind of parable; into the happiest stories there come warnings of coming danger, of

[4] Luke (5^{34}) has: 'Can you *make* them fast?' As a doctor he must have experienced the impossibility of inducing convivially-inclined people to fast.

[5] 'Be quiet; hold your tongues' (literally, 'Shut up and stay shut up!') would be a more exact, though less decorous, translation of our Lord's words in Mark 4^{39} than 'Peace, be still!'

tidal waves of destruction swooping down upon the homes of unwary sleepers, of burglars in the night, and darnel in the wheat, sinister suggestions of being left alone in the dark and of eternal fire; but meanwhile hindrances and forebodings are only mentioned, to be swept away on a tide of God's all-controlling and conquering power linked with man's triumphant faith, between them sweeping all obstacles out of their track.

When we turn to the parables about men and women, we become aware with what would be a shock if we are not so accustomed to these stories that we rarely let them play freely about minds, that we are not hearing much about prayer and still less about Church-going, or Sabbath-keeping, or the life of devotion, but rather about losing things and looking for them, about such mundane things as a poor man suddenly coming into money, or a ne'er-do-well son returning home in rags and the kind of welcome he got from his people, or as the misery of getting the sack from the office and looking for a job, about domestic difficulties and the law's delays, or the kindly stranger who is always ready to give first-aid when there is an accident on the roads, while the churlish fellow next door will not even bother to get up out of bed to help a friend in a difficulty. I wish I could ask the reader to tell me frankly what impression all this makes upon him. Is it all to be taken as read, and do we pass on to the green pastures of the Fourteenth Chapter of John? When all is said and done, what have we got here? What is there that is absolutely new? Something should be struggling to birth in our perhaps reluctant minds—reluctant because we all like our spiritual food served up on the dishes we are accustomed to. Jesus is telling us what God really feels about the jolly, easy-going people who haunt cinemas, football matches, and even dog-tracks, or the busy housewife who has all she can manage to keep up with 'make do and mend', with washing-days, and keeping her temper with restless children whom she must feed with inadequate rations, and queues, and having no help in the house—what He calls the 'worries about getting a living', in fact. Courage, good humour, compassion, ready friendliness, unpretentiousness, readiness to let bygones be bygones—where these are, as we can see them anywhere and any day of the week, there is the Kingdom of God, though they are far too common for us to pay much attention to them.

Jesus understood, as the prophets never did, how little the sins of private people have to do with public calamities. Even when He said, 'Except you repent, you shall all perish as they did' (Luke 13[3, 5])—the sternest warning He ever uttered to people without official responsibility—it is clear from the context that He did not mean 'Unless you mend your ways, you shall all go to perdition', but 'Unless you forgo your passion for revolt against Rome, you will be involved in unrelieved disaster'. All this does not mean that He had any illusions about humanity, but that He did not believe that men could be won to a better way of life by exhortation, but only by His companionship, by being shown something better in the only way they could see it, in practice. And it is surely obvious that our only way of weaning men and women away from drink and gambling and illicit sexual indulgence is by giving them something better *and more interesting* to think about—not primarily by warning them of that danger. The *only* individual of whom our Lord ever spoke contemptuously was Herod Antipas, and that was probably because of the way in which he had treated the Baptist, for in the Middle East the 'fox' (or rather 'jackal') has always been the symbol, not so much of slyness, but of wanton destructiveness. Moreover, Herod could not be called one of the common people.

This liking for human nature for its own sake—'warts and all'—not merely for the sake of making something different of it—and especially for what we call 'character' (by 'character' I do not mean virtue, but individuality or having a mind of one's own), is not the same thing as philanthropy. We should all agree without a quiver of our minds that Jesus was and is the 'lover of man's soul'; what I want to bring out is something quite different from this, though related to it. Let us say that He enjoyed people; the free companionship of men and women was congenial to Him, and He revelled in having them about Him, as St. Francis loved having birds and beasts about his cell. But with Jesus it is always 'How much *better* are you than birds!' or 'Is not a man *better* than a sheep?' Some poets and novelists since His time have shown the same delight in human nature, for its own sake, almost any sort of human nature, if it is content to be itself—Shakespeare, for instance (though his sympathy has rigid limitations), Dickens in his best moods, and Priestley in his homelier vein.

That Jesus was also an uncompromising realist, as we should have expected—if for no other reason than the fact that He had lived for thirty years and more in a small village—is proved, if proof were needed, by such passages as: 'If you then, *being evil*, know how to give good gifts to your children' or 'From within, out of man will come poisonous thoughts, fornications, thefts, murders, adulteries, knaveries, fits of malice, treachery, indecency, jealousy, scandal, arrogance, perversion' (Mark 7[21ff.]); love is *not* blind: it can be satisfied by nothing else than the truth.[6] Yet with all His heart and soul Jesus liked men and women, and only came near to despairing of them when they had made something inhuman of themselves, that is, when they were less than half alive. In this sense also, while there is life there is hope. So, in dealing with the sinner he would never probe more deeply than was necessary to bring a man or woman vividly to life, saying to one woman nothing more about her sins except that they were 'many' and that they were 'forgiven', giving to another—perhaps a less sensitive type—a résumé in greater detail of the kind of life she was living, but never alluding to the matter again in the course of a fairly long conversation—even then making friends with her first, and only then broaching the subject of sin at all. Moreover, to people like the Samaritan woman and Zaccheus, He was the first to make overtures and was quite willing to put Himself under an obligation to them—He was a poor man, and, if they could give Him nothing else, they could give Him charity—though the kind of life they had been living must have brutalized and coarsened them. And through it all He maintained the human footing, never adopting the role of a superior or moral reformer out to do good, though they would have readily accorded either to Him, if that would have kept Him at a safe distance. The First evangelist brings out the fact that while others—even the disciples on the one hand and the scribes on the other—learned to 'approach' him guardedly, the 'sinners'[7] and the children simply 'came'; indeed, the publicans

[6] In 1 Corinthians 13 Paul is giving us by implication his characterization as well as his life of Jesus, and we could not have a better guide. Here feminine and virile traits are perfectly balanced.

[7] 'Sinner' was a technical term then, as it is coming to be now. It stood generally either for sexual misconduct or co-operation with the occupying power (Rome or the Herods), regarded by public opinion as treasonable (a parallel can be found in our talk of 'social sins' and the phrase 'living in sin'). It is curious that moderns who explain personal sin away, by psychological and other means, stil lhold forth about

came 'and lay down' with Jesus—they were quite at home with our Lord and His disciples (Matthew 9[10]).[8]

In this matter, as in so many others, our Lord stands alone. He could never have said, like Paul, 'I would rather die than take your money' (1 Corinthians 15). As a matter of fact, the apostle did not finish his sentence, perhaps because he was aware that he could not justify his attitude by the example of Jesus. In any case, there is a palpable difference here, not to be accounted for by all the differences between Galilee and Corinth! Most English people's sympathies would probably be with Paul on this point, for we admire a determination to stand on one's own feet and pay one's own way; it is quite another question whether he would not have won the confidence of his flock at Corinth and kept it more surely if he had pocketed his pride, and allowed them to maintain him! Jesus, on the other hand, was above what we call 'proper' pride; he seems to have been perfectly willing to accept invitations to dinner at the houses of people whose only idea in asking Him was to snub this upstart prophet (Luke 7[44]). In a far truer sense than Paul could ever be, He was 'all things to all men'.

Saints like St. Francis have disdained the amenities of life or, like Father Damien, lived with lepers—but Jesus was no ascetic. There are signs that He was 'angry' with a man who, according to Luke, was 'full of leprosy' (Mark 1[41], in the 'Western' text, reads 'being angry' instead of being 'moved with compassion' and most textual critics agree now that this is almost certainly the original reading); we may, if we will, interpret it as meaning that He was angry with the leprosy, or that His anger was roused by the word 'if' ('If Thou wilt, Thou canst make me clean'), or (perhaps more correctly) that what looked like an angry gesture, was really an involuntary shudder; but, in any case, He touched him. There we have the picture; no insensitiveness, certainly no pleasure in defiance of convention or sanitary precautions, but abhorrence and compassion inextricably blended together.

'social' sins. In Luke 13[2] 'sinners' means rebels against Rome, and though the word is used by Peter of himself in Luke 5[8], this is an exception, and it is likely that Luke does not so accurately reflect Palestinian ideas as native-born evangelists. The word 'sin', on the other hand, kept its original meaning.

[8] Another group, not counting the children (Matthew 19[14]), who 'come' to Jesus, are the disciples of the Baptist after their master's death: this is significant of much for, a little while before, they had been critical of His feasting while John was in prison (Mark 2[18], Matthew 14[12]).

The importance of all this lies in the fact that we are not here concerned with tracing in detail the outlines of a perfect human character; this, if it was indeed true of Jesus of Nazareth, is a revelation of the heart of God, for 'He that hath seen' Him 'hath seen the Father'. The fundamental belief about man which the Bible, from beginning to end, is designed to express, is that man is 'made in the image of God and after His likeness', and this cannot mean less than that so far as we fail before our course in this world is run, and while we are associated with other people in the body, to approach (as far as with our imperfect knowledge and limited faculties we can) *God's* attitude toward our fellow men, we are running counter to the laws of our own being, and can never be mentally, morally, or spiritually healthy—and Jesus shows what that attitude was and is.

We can never hope to be as brave or as patient as He, if only because we shall never have so much to dare or endure; nor, of course, can we expect to be sinless, for we have stained our honour and compromised ourselves in a thousand ways. But we can practise some of His virtues; we can train ourselves in tolerance and humility. It is the more necessary that we, who have engaged ourselves to represent Him, should do so, for the only people He found fault with persistently and with most vehement indignation were the unforgiving—and refusal to forgive is at bottom the outcome of pride—the censorious and the self-satisfied. The word translated 'hypocrite', so often reported as coming from His lips, we are told by experts in Semitic languages, comes from a word which means 'irreligious'; it implies that a man is acting as though he were God presiding at the Last Judgement. The scribes had sat 'in Moses' seat' so long that they had come to look upon others than themselves as mere subject-matter for their reforming energy—in other words, as 'cases'; they were 'this people that knows not the law' (John 7[49]). Simon the Pharisee expressed their spirit when he muttered, 'This man, if He were a prophet, would have known who and what kind of woman this is who is touching Him, for she is a sinner'; he is summing up everybody in sight, putting both Jesus and the woman in their places (Luke 7[39]).

This is a terribly easy habit for morally earnest people to get into. A minister, overwhelmed by small personal problems among his people, may get into the way of summing them up to himself —'She is always making trouble', 'He likes the limelight', 'He has a bee in his bonnet', and so on. All the things he says may be true, and if he only lets them out at home, and when he is more than usually tired, and at other times manages to see something likeable about them, he is not likely to do himself or them much harm, but if he forms the habit of entering up his people in categories of this—or any—sort, he would do well to read again such passages from the Gospels as the story of the woman taken in adultery, for he is well on the way to be found standing where the scribes in that story stood in the presence of Jesus. Our Lord had certainly no romantic notions about the sins of the flesh but, unless the evidence of all three Synoptic Gospels is wholly misleading, He thought it necessary to warn men about the danger of sins of jealousy, pride, ambition, and self-satisfaction combined—as they generally are—with censorious criticism of other people ten times oftener and much more than ten times more incisively than about those sins we are thinking about when we mourn publicly over the degeneracy of the times. This is not rhetorical moralizing; it is a fact which any one of us can discover for himself. And if that is true we are not concerned with the ethical ideals of Christianity—whatever they are—but with the word and judgement of Almighty God. If this is really true, what are we to make of our endless discussions about the *authority* of the ministry? I, for one, can find no relevance in them whatever to anything that really matters.

I wonder, too, and increasingly, what bearing a fresh and open-minded examination of the teaching and example of our Lord is likely to have on some of the pronouncements that are so fashionable now to the effect that the events of the last few decades have exposed once and for all the modern heresy of humanitarian progress. The world lies under the judgement of God, we are told, and we must preach repentance. Yes—but *how* are we to preach it? I should feel happier about these sweeping assertions if I were not made to feel, every time I read the Gospels again, that our Lord's own emphasis was entirely different. He preached judgement, *not* to the world, but to the very people who were most ready to deplore its degeneracy. I have no difficulty in finding the note so much desiderated in the prophets, and even in Paul and John (in the First Epistle) —see Romans $3^{11\text{ff.}}$, 1 John 5^{19}—but it is significantly rare in the teaching of Jesus. It is not that he denied universal sinfulness

—in fact, He assumed it—but that He *did not take that line* in appealing to sinful men or women. And, if He is our final authority both for the manner and the matter of our preaching, we have no business to talk as though the last few decades have brought to light any facts about human nature of which He was not aware. What the last hundred years has shown more clearly perhaps than all the centuries before is that no man or group of men is fit to be trusted with absolute power over the lives of others, and that gifts of leadership are the most dangerous of all human faculties. That leaders and led may both fall into a ditch and drag a whole generation with them is plain enough, and it is also evident that our Lord's ideal was that the leader should use his influence to bring the disciple up to his own level, and so abolish as speedily as possible the dangerous superiority of conscious leadership (Luke $6^{39f.}$). But there is not really much substance in the assertion constantly made from the modern pulpit that the sins usually called vices of ordinary people are responsible for the world-wide tragedies of the last few years. The average man, if there is such a thing, may become immeasurably worse, or—perhaps more rarely—show himself substantially better under the inhuman provocations incidental to war; but he is never, or very seldom, as bad as all that. And, even in the case of the war-makers—whoever they were—we should do well to use the words of Jesus, when He said of His murderers, 'Father, forgive them, they know not what they do', and leave them to the judgement of God. This word of Jesus is not only the most charitable thing that was ever said on the subject, but it stands the test of the years as no other verdict on historical events has ever done. The more the truth comes to light, the clearer it becomes that those who make wars never know what they are doing.[9]

It may be said that the teaching of Jesus only gives half the picture; we must include in our view the vital fact that the very human nature in which Jesus believed so strongly let Him down in the end; the fact of the Cross is the final proof of the corruption of the human heart; Paul's doctrine of universal sinfulness

[9] When Paul wished to give a thoroughly pessimistic description of human nature (Romans $3^{10ff.}$), he has to go to one of the gloomiest of the Psalms for his authority; he knows he has no 'word of the Lord' behind him here. We might, if we chose, set against it another Old Testament quotation—also used by Paul in Romans (11^{4})—but this only shows that the game of hurling proof-texts at one another seldom gets us much farther.

is not based on the teaching of our Lord, but on the total impression made by the Cross, interpreted in the light of the apostle's own experience (Romans 7). If the parable of the Prodigal Son had told the whole story, there would have been no need of the Atonement for the sense of need would have been enough to drive men back to God.

It is true, of course, that the parables about men and women and their doings do not tell the whole story of human life. Indeed, they are all, perhaps deliberately, left without an ending, happy or otherwise. We should have liked to know how the prodigal son settled down at home, and whether the two brothers were reconciled after a while. We do not know whether the tenants of the estate from the control of which the unjust steward was dismissed *did* receive him into their homes after all, whether the man picked up by the Good Samaritan survived and, if he did, whether he ever troubled to thank his benefactor.[10] If these are—as has been argued persuasively—true stories, they must have ended somehow. But our curiosity is not satisfied, the reason perhaps being that the very essence of these stories is the taking of a real risk, and so the issue is still in the balance when the story comes to a close. In this they are, of course, true to actual life, for securely happy endings occur seldom except in fiction. And, because the life of the Son of God in the days of His flesh was an actual human life, the fact that He 'believed all things', and 'hoped all things' meant that He, too, had to 'endure all things', and among them all the chances and changes incident to dealings with men and women. It is not so with His parables of nature; they end with the harvest when the sickle can be put in, the work completed, and the story finished—for that year at any rate. If our Lord could have always been as sure as He was sometimes that He would 'draw all men' to Himself, the path He had to follow to its goal might have been painful but not heartbreaking, for it would have been only a question of lasting out. But He had other moods, as when He asked Himself whether He could reach lost souls from the other side of death, or whether He was going to find faith on the earth (Luke 16[30f.], 18[8]).

Here we may pause to point out that the question, 'How far were the rank and file of the Jewish people directly responsible

[10] That Jesus expected His patients to glorify God, if not to thank Him personally, is clear from the story of a grateful Samaritan (Luke 17[18]).

for the crucifixion of our Lord?', needs re-examination, for the Gospels are not unanimous. The first two Gospels take the darker view, while the last two give us a somewhat less gloomy picture. We will take the latter first. A close study of the Johannine Passion-story has convinced me that, in the Fourth Gospel, the common people are, by implication, acquitted, for, from the beginning to the end of the trial-scene, nothing is said about the presence either of non-official inhabitants of Jerusalem or pilgrims to the feast from Galilee. The trial takes place at six o'clock in the morning not, as we should gather from the Synoptic accounts, about eight (John 19^{14}).[11] The use of the word 'Jews' in the Fourth Gospel has misled most of its readers, and been responsible for much anti-Judaism in the Church. All through this Gospel the word 'Jews' stands for the people who in the other Gospels are called 'chief-priests' or 'elders' and 'scribes', that is, Pharisees and Sadducees holding more or less exalted official positions. It is impossible to conceive of the Jewish people *en masse* carrying on theological arguments such as are reported in chapter after chapter of the Fourth Gospel; no doubt they looked on and listened, but the protagonists—always called the 'Jews'—must have been highly-educated Rabbis. In John 18 and 19 the 'crowd', so prominent in the Synoptics, is *never once* mentioned, and in 19^{6} it is the 'chief-priests and their attendants' who shout 'Crucify, crucify!'

Turning to Luke's Gospel, it should be noticed that the women of Jerusalem are weeping for Him as He goes out to His death, and—still more significantly—when all is over, the crowd of spectators return home beating their breasts (Luke $23^{27, 48}$). The general public are represented here as 'looking on' (Luke 23^{35}) all through, knowing only too well that yet another outrage has been perpetrated, but not seeing what they could do about it; the rulers of the world had disposed of John the Baptist, and now they had finished with Jesus of Nazareth: what a world it was, to be sure!

In Mark's Gospel, on the other hand (15^{8}), the 'crowd' comes up to court, apparently after the trial has begun, to demand the release of a prisoner which Pilate has promised them. They had

[11] The view that the Fourth Evangelist uses Roman time (except when Palestinians are speaking, as in John 4^{52}) is now generally accepted; otherwise we are faced with a direct contradiction as to the hour of crucifixion between the Synoptic Gospels and the Fourth (compare John 19^{14} with Mark 15^{25}).

already been incited by secret agents of the chief-priests to shout for Barabbas.[12] Of course, Mark may well be right; we can easily imagine a sudden revulsion of public opinion against Jesus and in favour of Barabbas, who had at least put up some kind of a fight against Pilate, Herod, and Rome, especially when it became known—and we may be sure that the chief-priests' agents would see that it was made known widely—that Jesus of Nazareth had surrendered without a show of resistance the night before, and that money had changed hands over the affair. If that was the case, many of them would come up to court in a resentful mood, and the fact that Pilate was obviously hoping and expecting that they would shout for Jesus of Nazareth would be enough—such is human nature—to turn them against Him. This fact—if it is a fact—is quite compatible with an equally violent reaction when the deed was done

But the strongest statement implicating the general public in the judicial murder of our Lord is usually found in Matthew 27[25], which reads: 'Then all the people answered and said, His blood be upon us, and upon our children.' But what is meant by 'all the people' (not, it should be noticed, by 'all the crowds')? The change from the 'crowds' of verse 17 must be significant, for the 'people' and the 'crowds' are distinguished throughout the Gospels. The 'people' stand everywhere else for what we should call the 'Church', the 'crowd with the disciples' for the followers of Jesus not counted among the twelve, and the 'large crowd' or the 'crowds' for the mass of the population.

A reasonable inference from the evidence at our disposal would perhaps be to the effect that the chief instigators of the attack upon Jesus were the chief-priests and their underlings (a comparatively small group which was inflamed against Him by His cleansing of the Temple and His prophecy of its approaching destruction), that they seduced Judas Iscariot—who, as his second name suggests, may well have been fanatically devoted to the Temple—intimidated Pilate, and *may* have induced vociferous members of the zealot party, disappointed with Jesus because they thought He had let them down and gone over to the occupying power to shout for Barabbas, but that the general public were only to blame in so far as no one had the courage to make

[12] Whose name, according to the oldest version of Matthew 27[17], was also 'Jesus', and also 'Son of the Father', for that is what 'Barabbas' means; he was probably a son of a Rabbi, who had gone over to the extreme nationalist party.

any kind of effective protest.[13] It is extremely difficult to see how anyone could, for if an attempt to set Jesus free by force had been made, He would have been the first to suppress it! The chief-priests were concerned for their position, and possibly for their revenues;[14] Pilate was torn between fear of public disturbance—which would have ruined his official career—and fear of what his wife would say to him when he returned home;[15] nationalists were honestly bewildered by the persistent refusal of Jesus to follow up His cleansing of the Temple; the general public were either apathetic or too busy with their own affairs to do anything about it. And how true to life all this is! There is no hint in the Gospels that Jesus felt Himself let down by anyone but Judas. What He actually says is that *He* was letting His disciples down—in a sense—in Mark 14[27]. That the eleven forsook Him is true, but had not He told them that they could not 'follow Him now', and rebuked Peter for his attempt to defend Him? He certainly had not encouraged them, that night at least, to do anything else. What we really mean when we say that sinful human nature crucified our Lord, is that everything that had happened since the fall had made some such tragedy inevitable when He became incarnate, that the Lamb had indeed been slain since the foundation of the world. Even so, He would probably not have been *crucified*, if He had not violently cleansed the Temple.

Still, though He knew very well that His ministry could not last long in a world such as this, as passages like Mark 2[20] testify, there are too many suggestions of disappointment in His recorded words—disappointment, not so much perhaps with individual people, as with the generation to which He came—for us to say outright that He never hoped for a nation-wide response which was not eventually forthcoming. Such sayings as Matthew 12[45] =Luke 11[24], with its vivid picture of moral reformation under the leadership of the Baptist followed by swift relapse, or Matthew 11[16f.]=Luke 7[31f.] with its comparison of His generation to sulky children, or—still more strikingly—His woes on the Galilean

[13] Except Peter, and his protest cannot be called effective, nor was he one of the general public.

[14] Though it is only fair to say that Dr. Abrahams argued strongly that they got no direct *personal* profit from the sale of cattle in the court of the Gentiles.

[15] There is no reason why the First evangelist's testimony should not be accepted here, from what we know of Claudia who was related, we are told, to the imperial house.

towns and His heartbroken cry over Jerusalem are too well attested and too sweeping in their application to be ignored. There is an unmistakable change in His outlook which shows itself clearly enough in His parables. His rejection at Nazareth cannot have been a surprise, at least if the description of the tone of His address given there in Luke 4²³*ff.* [16] is to be accepted as it stands, but there is a perceptible change of atmosphere between Mark 5 and 7, which seems to be coincident with the death of John, and the attempt to make Jesus Himself King (see John 6¹⁵) after the feeding of the five thousand. Perhaps the crisis suggested by Matthew 11²⁰ᶠᶠ·=Luke 10¹⁷ᶠᶠ·, a passage which comes from 'Q', may be associated with the same period, but in this case it should be noticed that Jesus only turns from one constituency to another, from the 'quick-witted and shrewd' townspeople to the 'weary and heavy-laden' land-workers of the villages. It cannot have been long after this, however, before He left Galilee altogether, and it would appear that His campaign in the villages round Nazareth also proved disappointing. If we can rely upon the general outline of the order of events traced in Mark's Gospel it was then that He began to talk about rejection and death. At any rate, our Lord's *public* ministry involved Him in a series of frustrations; the Church in Jerusalem first, and afterwards in Galilee, the industrial populations by the crowded lakeside, and His own folk in the highlands, all let Him down in turn. How far this was due to the fact that the country was seething with political and social unrest it is hard to say, but it is at least clear that His difficulty in dealing with the most obstinate people in the Roman world[17] was exasperated by the 'spirit of the age', as our difficulties are today.

Yet most of us are well aware that it is possible to meet disappointment at every turn in our *public* work, and still find great satisfaction in our private relations with individual men and women; a 'generation' may be unresponsive, while many of the

[16] Some scholars think that two visits to Nazareth have been telescoped into one in this chapter. Certainly the somewhat combative tone of verses 23ff. seems out of keeping with 'All bore Him witness and wondered at the words of grace which came out of His mouth'. It is possible, however, that after a promising beginning, Jesus became aware of an undercurrent of criticism, and decided to deal with it at once.

[17] In the Roman Empire at that time Jews had the same kind of reputation as the Irish gloried in when they were under British rule—bonny fighters, but the most awkward and obstinate nation in the world.

individuals who belong to it may, by their kindness and appreciation, help to keep our faith in human nature alive. When, because we feel we ought to understand our times, we make ourselves read one of the 'debunking' novels—to use an ugly name for a still uglier thing—which pour out of the Press in our days, we wonder where these novelists have been living, for we look round on our neighbours and can find nothing remotely resembling the life they describe. Everywhere round us, among Church-goers and outsiders alike, we meet decency, helpfulness, and—more often than not—generosity, and are indebted constantly to people (on whom we have no kind of special claim) for services of all kinds. Why must men be for ever fouling their own nests? If preachers and theologians join in the cats' chorus, and we have to listen to it in Church, there will be no escape for us! The fact that Jesus said 'The Son of Man has not where to lay His head' has led many Gospel-readers to assume that He met nothing but hostility from the cradle to the Cross, but a moment's consideration would convince us that it cannot have been so. When Mary had to lay her infant Son in a manger, because there was no room for Him in the living-room[18] of the house where they were stranded, we may be sure that no Jewish people would have allowed either mother or child to lack anything that they could provide; whatever else can be said against them in other respects, they have never been wanting in care for motherhood, or love for children. And there are many signs that it was so all through. He was able to send out His twelve without any provision for the journey with no likelihood of their going short of food or shelter; perhaps He could not have done so in London, but He probably would in the English countryside. Such casual notices as that 'women ministered to Jesus of their substance' (Luke 8³), and that 'a woman named Martha received Him into her house' (Luke 10³⁸—there is no suggestion that Jesus and Martha had met before) are probably only typical of what must have been continually happening; and it seems likely that our Lord's travels as a holy man in Palestine were far less laborious and dangerous than Paul's in Asia Minor. It was true that He had no home *of His own*, and in that sense had

[18] The word used in Luke 2⁷ does not generally mean 'inn', but 'room in a house' (it is used of the upper room in Luke 22¹¹). For 'inn' another word is used in Luke 10³⁴. So the churlish innkeeper of the nativity plays should be allowed to disappear.

'nowhere to lay His head', and that He was 'numbered among the outcasts' at the end, but up till then there is no suggestion anywhere that He had any difficulty in obtaining hospitality anywhere except in Samaria, and, as Luke tells us, there were particular reasons in that case (9^{53}); even then He had only to go on to another village (verse 56).

Apart from the twelve and the devoted women who followed Him on His last journey to Jerusalem, Mark tells us that there was generally 'a crowd along with His disciples' (see 8^{34}, 9^{15}, etc.), and it seems likely that He left behind Him a considerable following in Galilee when He set off for His last journey to Jerusalem.[19] To what extent the very numerous people whom He had healed and helped in various ways became His attached followers we have no means of knowing, and apart from two or possibly three publicans among the twelve, we cannot be certain that many publicans actually followed Him for long. But the fact that there was such an ingathering after the Resurrection seems to imply that our Lord's ministry had been far more successful among the general body of the public, and especially in Jerusalem, than has generally been supposed. Even if the figures Luke gives us are exaggerated (and five thousand male converts in a few weeks certainly seems a large number—see Acts 2^{41} and 4^{4}),[20] there must have been a sensational influx into the Church to account for the feebleness of the authorities in dealing with the movement in contrast with their high-handed action against its Leader only a short time before and in the same city. It is not often realized how completely the fact that Jesus had been seen by most people in Jerusalem to have died on a cross would paralyse any movement in His favour, and that for the time being the fact that He had *not* been delivered from a death on which God had set His curse in Scripture (Deuteronomy

[19] It has been suggested with much plausibility that the 'apostles' who, in 1 Corinthians 15^{7}, are clearly differentiated from the twelve, were delegates sent by James, the Lord's brother (the appearance to whom has just been mentioned) to followers and friends of Jesus who had not gone up to Jerusalem to the feast, and who would not have heard of the Lord's resurrection. The sudden emergence of this James into prominence after the Resurrection may well be due to the fact that Jesus had appointed him His liaison officer with them.

[20] 'Five thousand *men*', says Luke in 4^{5}. It may probably be assumed that the women outnumbered the men. It is not necessary, of course, to add the 3,000 of 2^{41} to the 5,000 of 4^{4}. It is quite likely that in Acts 2–4 we have *two* accounts of the way in which the revival began, with varying computations of the number of converts. For the Jewish custom of not counting women and children separately, see Matthew 14^{21} and 15^{38}.

21[23]) would seem, to friend and foe alike, to dispose of His claim to be the Messiah. That so many people—including many *priests* (Acts 6[7]—Luke's expression is very strong)[21]—were ready to take Peter's word for it that Jesus of Nazareth had risen from the dead speaks volumes for the impression that He had made upon them, especially if the priests were Sadducees, who were generally agnostics on the whole subject of the future life! Some such popular backing must have been given to the new movement to account for its establishment in the very city which had witnessed its complete collapse, and this cannot be accounted for except by the influence exerted by Jesus Himself on *all* classes. Even in the case of the Pharisees, the remark of James, the Lord's brother, in Acts 21[20] is significant. It runs: 'You see, brother, how many myriads there are among the Jews of those who have become Christians, *and all of them are zealots for the law.*' The word 'myriads', which originally meant 'ten thousands', had come simply to mean 'any number of' by this time and, unless James was exaggerating wildly—and Paul makes no attempt to qualify his statement—our Lord's attentions even to the Pharisees had been by no means wasted.

Our inference should, I think, be that in an intelligible attempt to do justice to the importance of what happened at Pentecost, Christian historians have unconsciously minimized the abiding results of our Lord's own work. He must have been far more successful in winning His fellow-countrymen than a hasty reading of the Gospels would suggest; if it were not so, we should be forced to the conclusion that His prophecies (as in the parable of the dragnet) of miraculous ingathering had not been fulfilled. For the moment, the mood of the times made the nation as a whole unresponsive to His message, but with hundreds, if not thousands, this greatest of all experts in the art of fishing for men succeeded, though it was a case of gradual, not instantaneous, transformation—'First the blade, then the ear, then the full corn in the ear', as He said. And, even if the new movement which He started ebbed away from the shores of Palestine (and, after a century or so, made a fresh start overseas), the people who carried it there were very largely Palestinian disciples of Jesus; Paul was, of course, a notable exception, but he *was* an exception —if his case had not been abnormal, he would not have had to

[21] He says: 'The mass of the priests'!

fight so hard for recognition as an apostle. He said himself that he was an 'anomaly' (1 Corinthians 15[8]).

Who founded the Churches in Rome, Alexandria, Syrian Antioch, the largest cities in the Empire? We cannot be sure of their names, though we may be allowed to guess at some of them (Acts 11[20]), but they were certainly *not* converts of Paul. Jews who accepted the message of Jesus were only a 'remnant' of a large population, it is true, but there is no reason to suppose that they were a negligible minority.[22]

But what has all this to do with parables? If our Lord did, during a ministry of less than three years' duration, lay the foundations of a movement which has so completely changed the course of the history of civilized mankind that we count our years from His birth, it must be true that, not merely the facts of His death and reported Resurrection, or the beliefs about His person and mission which came to be entertained by vast numbers of people, but also such clues as His recorded words give us as to His intentions and policies must be given due weight. This is to put the matter from the historian's point of view, but for convinced Christians there can surely be no question about the matter; they will listen to every word He said as closely as to the story of what He did.

He began with the declaration that God was at work in a new way in the life of His people, not with any eschatological or political programme of religious or social revolution. The Baptist's preaching, resulting as it had done in the first real mass-movement of moral and religious reformation since the history of Israel began,[23] had aroused a lively spirit of expectation in the popular mind, while His own healings of the minds and bodies of men and women confirmed our Lord's conviction that the 'Kingdom of God' had already come. Then, quite suddenly, He seems to have changed His tactics; He 'began to speak in parables', and at the same time to manifest a tendency to concentrate upon the training of a small group of disciples. Mark, the earliest of our evangelists, seems to have thought that

[22] Such statements as John 12[19, 42] should not be left out of account in the general picture. They make it clear that, *before the Resurrection*, the influence of Jesus, even in Jerusalem, was strong enough to induce in the minds of the authorities something like panic.

[23] The reformation under Josiah was engineered by authority, and the new start after the Exile was the work of a comparatively small band of returned captives.

He had come to doubt the efficacy of preaching, and was banking rather upon gradual processes than quickly visible results, and there is a good deal in the earlier parables to suggest that this was indeed the case. We should rather say that from the beginning He realized that any lasting success must depend on permanent qualities implanted by God in human nature (Mark $4^{26ff.}$), for God works in the same way in nature and in grace, not by the earthquake and the tornado in nature (though they have their function), but by qualities in the soil, the seasons, the sunshine and the rain, and in human nature, not by sensational revolutions in public opinion, or emotional crises, but by the processes by which men as God made them are brought, by example and experience, to recognize their utter dependence upon God, that is, to 'faith'.[24] In the parable about men and women to which the parables about nature lead up, we see the ground on which God sets about working His miracles of grace.

In both spheres, in nature and in human life alike, God works quietly, using as the media of His creative and redemptive energies: in nature, such things as the movement of the seasons, properties hidden in the soil and the seed, the sunshine and the rain; in human life the willingness to forgive and forget, the humility, the readiness to take risks, the persistence and perseverance in the face of difficulty, the unassuming friendliness, good humour and tolerance, and, above all, the neighbourly compassion characteristic of most of the men and women we meet in the train and the bus, in shopping queues and the office, as well as in Church. Much more attention should be paid to the character-sketch of our Lord in Matthew $12^{18ff.}$ (it is not a mere quotation from the Servant Songs of Isaiah 42–53), for it gives us the clue not merely to the methods of Jesus, but also to those of God.[25] The parables tell us what Jesus thought was most divine in human nature. These qualities do not of themselves create the 'faith' upon which Jesus lays so much emphasis, but they not only provide the conditions which make faith possible, the soil in which the seed of grace may grow, but the fact that their friends possess them makes faith easier for men and women not themselves so

[24] 1 Kings $19^{11ff.}$ may be taken as a commentary on this.

[25] These are two ways of saying the same thing, of course, but it is important to notice that, in most of His parables, Jesus is not thinking of Himself at all, but of God's dealings with men in general.

richly endowed with these qualities.[26] His own coming brought them into active exercise, as the sun quickens the soil, but they were already there.

All the parables about people show us either the presence or absence of these qualities in the characters depicted, and the healing miracles tell the same tale. The woman with the haemorrhage showed persistence and refusal to give up hope, though the life she must have been living for twelve years must have been as depressing as any woman's could be; the centurion showed compassion for his slave; the Syro-Phoenician quickness of wit and refusal to take offence; the father of the epileptic boy determination to grapple with and conquer his doubts; the blind man who let himself be taken for a walk in the dark by a stranger, away from the village where he could find his way home or get someone to help him if he was left stranded, willingness to take risks; and so on.

The Temptation-story, itself an acted parable, shows Jesus refusing to take the easy way of doing something *for* men instead of *with* them. He might have appealed to their hunger for food or excitement, or He might have pandered to their congenital weakness by compromise (which He calls devil-worship), but He resolved rather to trust their God-implanted strength. Doing so, He might lose the first and the second battle, but He knew He would win in the end. Perhaps the greatest thing in the Gospel-story is the proof it gives us that, in spite of everything, God believes in the essential goodness of man's human nature, and so should we.

Someone said (I think it was R. L. Stevenson, but cannot trace the reference): 'I intend to go on praising the English climate till I die, even though I know it will be the death of me.' I quote this because it expresses better than my words can the attitude of our Saviour to 'us men and our salvation'. He knew all there is to know about the poison that has found its way into every nook and cranny of our human life, infecting every good thing about us and in us, and He was well aware that before very long really sharing our life He would have to drink the bitter cup of trust betrayed and love rejected which so many men and women

[26] A good example of this can be found in the story of the four men who brought the paralysed man to Jesus; the 'faith' of the men who brought him expressed itself in persistence in face of difficulty, and it spread to the man whom they carried ('Jesus, seeing *their* faith'—Mark 2^5).

have had to drink. But we may reverently say that it was infinitely worth His while—perhaps we can hardly make too much of the phrase which, on His last night spent with His friends before His passion, lingered on His lips: 'Those whom Thou hast given Me out of the world' (John 17[6, 24], etc.), or of the eagerness with which He grasped at the prospect of having a *man* with Him in Paradise (Luke 23[41ff.]). In dealing with sinful men and women, He does not probe and pry like a psychoanalyst; it is as though He said: 'Yes, I know, but let us say no more about it, and take it for granted that it is done with, now we have found each other' (see, for examples, Mark 2[7], Luke 5[8], and many more). Of course, the fact that He *could* do so is the best possible proof that He was divine, but surely it also suggests that Paul was right when he bade his converts 'take it for granted that they were dead to sin and alive unto God' (Romans 6[11]). There is no question of complacency here, only of a resolute refusal to be intimidated by evil either within or without, as Paul said again: 'Be not overcome by the evil, but overcome the evil with the good' (Romans 12[21]). This is good psychology as well as good religion and—more important than either—it was the way the Master of us all took with the individual sinner as well as with the evil in the world about Him.

It is perhaps even more significant that, in the parables which are brought together in Luke 15, His word for the man who has gone wrong is 'lost'. When Jesus speaks of 'the lost' (see Luke 19[10]), He does not mean primarily those who *feel themselves lost*—or, as we should say, frustrated, lost in the desert or in the crowd—but those whom their owners or their people have lost, like a lost sheep or coin or son. God's sorrow, not man's remorse, the gap in the family rather than the heinousness of the offence is always the leading consideration with Jesus. That is why the first essential was, not that they should be reformed, but that they should be *found*—God would do the rest. Jesus could not be content as, their modern apologists are ready to confess, the Rabbis were content, to welcome repentant sinners; He sought them out and did not cease to associate with them, though they showed no outward sign of changing their ways.

This must always be the distinguishing mark of Christian evangelism. We must live with people as they are, before we can hope to make them any different. It is significant that a real revival of religion is now spreading far and wide in industrial France, because hundreds of priests are being ordained, not to act as visiting chaplains in factories, but to work and take their pay and belong to the unions side by side with their workmates. Miners are being trained as priests, ordained, and then sent back to the mines, as engineers and so on. Whether this is practicable in our country with our divided Churches or not I gravely doubt, but *it is what Jesus Himself did.* He trained Himself by living for twenty years at least as a working man before, so far as we know, He opened His mouth to preach. If, as we say, England is now, to all intents and purposes, a heathen country, we must do as overseas missionaries do—live among the people and learn their language before we attempt to preach to them.

But we can see what was the inevitable outcome of this policy for Jesus, as it would almost certainly be its consequence for us. He became deeply involved, not in the sins of the people He trusted and loved so much, but in the results of them. At first He was sure of two things: one was that 'with God all things are possible', and the other that 'all things are possible' to 'faith'—there were then only two essential necessities, that God should be at work in any given situation, and that men should respond to Him. He had no use for the word 'if' in His vocabulary[27] in those days; afterwards, on the other hand, hesitation is implied, if not explicitly stated, most clearly in Gethsemane. To take another illustration—He had said, 'Whoever upsets one of these little people that believe in me, the best thing that could happen to him would be that a great millstone were hung about his neck, and he were sunk in the deep sea', out of the way of further mischief (Matthew 18[6]), but the time came when He Himself had to confess, 'You shall *all* be upset *by Me* tonight' (Matthew 26[31]), for in the complexities involved in living with men, good and evil are so tangled up together that no one of us can tell where one begins and the other leaves off, even in his own motives, much less in the world about him. That is why our choice must so often lie, not between good and evil, but between two evils. We have noticed already the secular tone of some of His parables; here we may observe that this is all the more

[27] On the two occasions on which people say 'if' to Him, Jesus protests at once. One says 'If you will' (Mark 1[40]), the other, 'If you can' (9[23]). In 14[36] Mark has 'All things are possible to Thee', with no 'if' clause which, however, appears in the form 'If it be possible' in Matthew 26[39], and in the form 'If Thou wilt' in Luke 22[42].

surprising because He had been brought up in an atmosphere of what we should call old-fashioned piety. If we can judge by the story told by Luke ($2^{41ff.}$) about His interview with the Rabbis in the Temple cloisters when He was a boy of twelve, His youthful admiration for the teachers of Israel as well as His devotion to the Holy City was intense. We should have expected this, but it makes the fact that, according to the Fourth Gospel, the next time He was there, He had a whip of small cords in His hand (John 2^{15}), all the more significant. A story like that of the Good Samaritan shows plainly that He had soon discovered what has bewildered many another boy brought up in the shelter of the Church, that the people who make no profession of religion at all often show virtues sometimes lacking in its declared devotees. The bewilderment created by this discovery is revealed also in the parable of the Two Sons (Matthew $21^{28ff.}$)—it would seem that the shock it expresses has affected copyists and expositors all down the centuries. The vehemence of the attack on the scribes in Matthew 23 cannot be understood without this background.

Side by side with the discovery that many of the men of light and leading in His Mother-Church had forgotten 'justice and mercy and truth' in their determination to maintain a reputation for strict living, the fact had to be faced that people like the Good Samaritan were lost to it. There is not the least suggestion in this story that its hero made any profession whatever of religion, and even in the parable of the Prodigal Son, the one mention of the name of God comes in the prodigal's confession, and then only in what had become in popular speech a conventional phrase, 'I have sinned to heaven' (that is, 'I am a very great sinner').[28] The unjust steward is one of the 'children of this world, yet he is described as 'wiser' than the 'children of the light'. Everyone praises God in the stories of healing—except the nine lepers—but that was because they had met Jesus. But when the prodigal son comes home, there is no praising God, but only 'dancing to the pipes'; these people are, to all intents and purposes, pagans, but what delightful people some of them are! All this is, surely, a record of experience, but our Lord's joy in their goodness must have been three parts pain to find such 'flowers of God's heart' lost to the Church of God. Why should they 'pass like weeds

[28] cf. Exodus 2^2 ('a child amiable to God') and Jonah 3^2 ('Nineveh, a city great to God').

away'? And what about the 'far country' in which these people must pass their days, with gangsters haunting the roads they must travel, human vampires who are ready to live on a country lad's money while he has any in his pocket, and send him to feed their swine when it is gone, corrupt magistrates, money-lenders, and rack-renting landlords, while poor men competed with snarling dogs in its streets for bits of dirty bread tossed into the gutters by their rich neighbours? Wild flowers grow over blitzed areas, but the ruins tell their squalid story all the same. And meanwhile the men with whom our Lord had so much in common, from whom He had learnt His first lessons in the word of God and habits of devotion, 'passed by on the other side'. They had enjoyed a real experience of God, and He told them that 'the Kingdom of God was within them' (Luke 17^{21}),[29] but how deeply it was buried! To be different (the word 'Pharisee' probably means 'separate')[30] from the 'people of the land' had come to be the be-all and the end-all of their religious life, their real devotion to the Church having become the drug which sent their souls to sleep. And all alike—Pharisee, yes, and most of those who were outside the synagogue, too—were satisfied, the Pharisees with the knowledge that, as our evangelical fathers used to say, 'they did not go with the giddy multitude to do evil', and the others that they were as good as the people who made such a song about their religion. Perhaps the Samaritan met the priest and Levite farther down the road, and found time while he was binding up the wounds of the gangsters' victim to reflect upon the fact that these hypocrites had left the poor fellow to his fate, for all their fine talk! What was needed on all hands was 'faith', but where was it to be found (Luke 18^{9})?

What, then, was this 'faith', to which Jesus attached such overriding importance? Not a virtue, like humility or compassion, or readiness to forgive and forget, for Jesus found these, as we have seen, on every side; but a state of mind. The people who came to Him for what they could get from Him, yet never, so far as we know, became His followers, often had it,[31] whereas the disciples who had left home to follow Him were called 'men

[29] For a discussion of this saying, see above, p. 23.

[30] Paul is playing on the word 'Pharisee' in Galatians 1^{15} ('He who *separated* me from my mother's womb').

[31] The Gentile centurion and the Syro-Phoenician woman had 'great faith'.

of little faith' and were asked 'How is it you have not got faith?'[32] It is a sense of desperate need, and without it it is impossible to please God; that is not because God requires from men abject submission or an acknowledgement, every time they approach Him, of their utter dependence—what human father would?—but because a man cannot become aware of God at all without this sense of need, without which he is merely concerned with thoughts and ideas about God, never with God Himself. In the Gospels, 'faith' stands not so much for the contents of a man's creed, as for the degree of his trust in God alone. Theoretically, the Pharisee trusted in God only—he said so in his daily prayers but, in fact, he trusted in his own record, his reputation, his knowledge, even, as the story of the Pharisee and the Publican shows, in his superiority to others. No doubt the faith of the people who came to Jesus for healing was rather in Him than consciously in God and, when they had got what they had wanted, it may sometimes have ceased to have any living power in their lives. Only His disciples, secret or declared, consciously *believed* that God was in Him, and they believed more strongly at some times than at others. Most of them were well-meaning young idealists who adored their Leader, but they had not yet lost confidence in themselves; indeed, they could not be said to be 'like little children' except in their occasional childishness; but at least they were on the way, and our Lord had no fears for all but one of them.

How far His resolution to go up to Jerusalem and undergo the last hazard there was dictated by simple obedience to a direct command of His Father, or to what extent it was the outcome of long reflection—whether, in other words, Jesus normally had to rely for His guidance, as we have, on a combination of circumstances interpreted by prayer and meditation and the study of the Scriptures, and did not wait for voices[33] from Heaven—we have no means of telling, but His own reported words make it clear that the Songs of the Suffering Servant of God (Isaiah 52-3) were much in His mind from the beginning to the end of this crisis (Mark 10^{45}, Luke 22^{37}). At least it is clear that, being who

[32] Like the rest of us except on special occasions; we trust in Christ for salvation, it is true, but in how many things (and people) for almost everything else!

[33] We only hear of two voices from Heaven addressed to Jesus, one at the beginning, and one at the end of His ministry (Mark 1^{11}, John 12^{28}), for the Voice at the Transfiguration was addressed to His disciples.

and what He was, He could not let either His people or the world go; He could not find complete satisfaction, however much joy the prospect of their companionship in a better world than this (John 14[3]) gave Him, in saving a few men and women whom His Father has already given Him out of the world, while the 'many' were left to drop out of any knowledge of, and fellowship with, His Father. He had never doubted, we may well believe, that He would ultimately win His battle of love, but what of the interim, of the people He had known, whom He had come to save from their sins? No sensitive spirit even among us can find much satisfaction in the contemplation of some far-off victory of the Cross; the people we are concerned with do not belong to some future generation—they are those we have known. So it must have been, with immeasurably greater intensity, with our Lord. He had done everything that deeds and words could do, and now the 'night was coming, in which no one could work' in the way He had worked. He had been taught that the spirits of saints and martyrs were active upon earth;[34] they were set free by the death of the body. If that was so, He too must die, and in Jerusalem (Luke 13[33]).

The cleansing of the Temple was a deliberate act of extreme provocation; Jesus knew that, providing the mob, as it did, with an excuse for a riotous assembly it would, in all human probability, lead directly to His crucifixion as a political revolutionary, which He certainly was not. The Romans would not tolerate riotous assembly, least of all at Passover.

Jesus was Himself responsible for the *manner* of His death, as well as the time and place at which it was to happen. The Fourth evangelist is our best guide to the reason of His choice (see John 10[18]). It was to be His 'glory', 'glory as of an only Son of the Father, full of grace and truth', as complete a revelation of the grace of God and the truth about man as was possible in a medium provided by the experience of the age in which His life in the flesh was lived. He knew, as He told His disciples when they brought Him the message from Greek-speaking Jews of the dispersion[35] which offered Him a chance of escape and a new

[34] 'No man has ever ascended into Heaven', we read in John 3[13]. This was now orthodox Jewish doctrine. Moses almost got there, and Elijah got even nearer. No doubt popular opinion held that not only Moses and Elijah, but also Enoch had been translated.

[35] That they are meant by 'Greeks' here is suggested by John 7[35].

start for the work to which He had dedicated Himself in another country, that He must die, and die in Jerusalem, if His work was to bear much fruit. The deep truth underlying all His parables about 'nature' and human nature alike had been that in this world of time and space all life comes only through a kind of death (John 12^{24}). The seed must die before the corn can grow, and the *risk* which we have found to be a feature common to all the stories told by Jesus that can be called, in the full sense of the word, 'parables', really implies the kind of living death which, in another phase of life, any woman must undergo before a child can be born (John 16^{21}). In a deeper sense than lies on the surface of the Burial Service, 'in the midst of life we are in death'.[36] Life itself is paradox through and through, and the most frequently repeated and best-attested paradox of the Gospels (six times over: twice in 'Matthew', once in Mark, twice in Luke, and once in 'John') is perhaps the final paradox in our human experience, which He shared. It is 'He that saveth his life shall lose it', etc.

But why, specifically, death upon a cross? Because it is not enough for a heavenly Messenger to come to us here in our prison-house of mortality, and say—however true what He says may be—'The Kingdom is here; all you need do is to "believe in the good news"; the gates are open, and the sun is shining outside them', for the prison in which we 'sit and hear each other groan' is our own self-consciousness, the only self we have to live with most of the time.

If we all died easily, it might have been enough for Him, as we say, to 'pass away'. Of all the deaths that the cruel ingenuity of men have contrived for each other, crucifixion carries with it perhaps the greatest intensity of pain and humiliation; the Cross had become indeed a symbol for all that was obscene and degrading, as Cicero said in a famous passage.[37] Hundreds of

[36] This is perhaps the meaning of the (so-called) 'curses' in Genesis $3^{16ff.}$, as also of such a strange passage as 1 Timothy 2^{15} ('She shall be saved through childbearing', —or (?) 'kept safe through child-bearing'). Death is at once the penalty of sin and the result of the fall of man and the way to salvation; our very surrender in any real conversion is a kind of death, for—in essence—death is nothing but letting ourselves go, because we can no longer *keep* ourselves alive, or hold on to ourselves.

[37] Of course, it is not suggested that Jesus chose the Cross simply because it was the worst kind of death which could be inflicted. He deliberately risked it, because He determined at all costs to make a protest against the traffic in the Court of the Gentiles, which stood for the fiercely and contemptuously nationalist spirit which was to be the ruin of His people. Though not a political revolutionary, He died the death meted out only to revolutionaries, rebels, and slaves.

his countrymen had perished on the cross—by allowing Himself to be nailed to the Cross He met two of them and saved one of them from despair. Whatever His motive, He has at once lifted the Cross from the deepest imaginable degradation to Heaven, and in the long run abolished crucifixion. As a boy of thirteen or so He had almost certainly watched some of His older contemporaries being crucified before the walls of Sepphoris,[38] and we can dimly imagine the ghastly impression the spectacle made on His mind.

We think of another of the world's famous martyrs, Socrates of Athens, put to death, like Jesus, for disturbing the minds of men and setting one generation against another (Luke 12[53]—see also the Marcionite additions in Luke 23[2], 'He destroys the law and the prophets' and 'estranges from us our wives and *our sons*') and undermining the moral sanctions. But what a difference! Socrates is eloquent in his own defence; Jesus silent. Socrates tells his fellow-citizens, when he leaves the court, 'You go your way, and I go mine; which is better the gods alone know', and, when his friend Crito asks 'How shall we bury you?', replies: 'You must catch me first.' If Luke's account of the transfiguration is to be trusted, Jesus thought at that time of His coming death as 'the exodus which He was about to accomplish in Jerusalem' (Luke 9[31]). We may be inclined to think that this sentence probably expresses rather the thoughts of the three disciples than that of Jesus—in any case, the whole point of the Passion story, in the Synoptics at least, was that there was *no exodus* for Jesus; He was not to escape from His Egypt as Moses did. He was caught, but only because He let Himself be taken by His pursuers. Nor was He, like Socrates, thinking of Himself, and what He was going to do when death was over; He had done that, for He had prophesied that He would rise 'after three days' (Mark 8[31]), but 'this was' their 'hour, and the power of the dark' (Luke 22[53]); up till then He had called it *His* hour, and almost exulted in its coming (John 17[1]). Socrates said at his trial that men are most prophetic when they are about to die; Jesus was finding His way across the barrier which His self-consciousness had built up between Him and the rest of us, and was now living the scene through with us. He half excuses Pilate for the sorry

[38] Josephus tells us that thousands of Galilean zealots were crucified by the Romans when Sepphoris was taken (A.D. 6–7), and Sepphoris was only a few miles from Nazareth.

part he played (John 19^{11}), and whereas the fact that the chief-priests and scribes would not be true to themselves, but were for ever playing a part, keeping up appearances for the sake of office or reputation, had almost led Him to despair of reaching them,[39] now He finds His consolation in the fact that 'they know not what they do' (Luke 23^{34}).[40] He is able to turn what He had called 'hypocrisy' inside out. If they had been disinterested in their misjudgement of Jesus, the prospect might have been hopeless; as it was, there was still a chance that some day they would discover the truth. The impression I get is that Jesus is more and more, as the hours go by, living in others; that in Gethsemane he was wrestling in agonized prayer for Judas and His own people ('Judas' means 'Jew'); that, as Pilate and the Gentile soldiers take their part in the story, even the fate of Jerusalem and the Jews is seen as part of the long tragedy of the ages. God will conquer, but alas for the centuries that must pass, the crucifixion of humanity in age after age! I believe it was P. T. Forsyth who said of Gethsemane that 'all the sorrow of the centuries surged through the soul of Jesus in that hour of mortal agony'. When the pain of it became so great that He was forced back in upon Himself again (we must not forget that He had refused the drug[41] which was offered Him when the crucifixion was complete) we do not know, but we know that intense physical pain drives the sufferer in upon himself away from all alleviating distractions. He had thought of His mother, of His murderers, of Pilate, the Priests and the soldiers, of Peter and Judas alike and, last of all, of the young revolutionary dying beside Him—now He comes back to Himself. A black wave of despair which He had held away at arm's length all His life and even in Gethsemane comes back upon Him again, and now He can hold it off no longer—He is fully 'God with us' at last. He has broken into our prison-house, sounded the heights and the depths of human experience; there is no state of forsakenness and despair in which any man can find himself on this side of the grave or

[39] Compare the tone of 'How are you to escape judgement to hell?' (Matthew 23^{33}) and 'Why do I talk to you at all?' (John 8^{25}).

[40] Acts 3^{17} shows that this was taken by Peter—or at least by Luke—as applying to their 'rulers'.

[41] 'Myrrhed wine' (Mark 15^{23})—if by myrrh is meant what we mean by the word—would be a stimulant, not a narcotic; perhaps the First evangelist's 'wine mingled with a bitter herb' (Matthew 27^{34}) is a correction as well as a reminiscence of Psalm 69^{21}. But 'myrrh' was used as a generic term for any spiced drink or scent.

the other that our Lord has not penetrated. Because He was man He could bear our sins and sorrows in His body to the Cross; because He is God—indeed most truly the God who alone of all persons in the universe can empty Himself, when His self-emptying was complete, and He cried, 'My God, My God, why hast Thou forsaken Me?'—He bore our sins away on the Cross, saving us, as God saves us, by just being there, by being made manifest.

This is the vision of God for which the disciples were being prepared by the washing of their feet; this is the coming of the Bridegroom for which all their life with Jesus had been a preparation. And it is not a vision of God only, but of the meaning of man's life, of his triumphs and failures alike. It is the acted parable to which all His other parables in words and deeds lead up and in which they find their explanation, the 'sign' of which His 'many other signs' are but a faint foreshadowing.

Now behold the Deity,
Now His heavenly birth declare!
Faith cries out: "Tis He, 'tis He!'
My God who suffers here.

Yes, and 'Behold the man', too; *ecce homo, ecce Deus*—God *with us* at last! There is a Cross in the heart of God, but it is a transfigured Cross, become the 'wondrous' Cross because it is lodged for ever there. A comparatively modern poet has written:

His folly has not fellow
Beneath the blue of day
That gives to man or woman
His heart and soul away.

The Gospel of the grace of God answers, 'Yet this is what the Son of God did, when He "emptied Himself" . . . and followed the path of obedience as far as death, yes, death upon the Cross. That is why God has greatly exalted Him, and given Him the name that is above every name, that, when the name of "Jesus" is pronounced, every knee in Heaven, on earth, in hell, should bow, and every tongue confess that Jesus Christ is *Lord Supreme*, to the glory of God the Father.' For, indeed, 'the folly of God is wiser than men'; what does 'emptying oneself' mean but giving heart and soul away? 'He that loses His life shall save it'—if He loses it as Jesus did.

'Hallelujah! *What a Saviour!*'

INDEX OF SUBJECTS

INDEX OF SCRIPTURE REFERENCES